Journey Subject To Change

Leo Stone

Artwork and cover design by Dissect Designs

ISBN: 978-1-0685159-1-0

DEDICATED TO

My girls.

The one who always held my hand and told me I could do it, when I didn't believe in myself.

And the one who never got the chance to hold my hand.

Never Here, But Always There.

Journey Subject To Change

A collection of poems for those of us who feel things that little bit deeper, and who despite all indications to the contrary, are determined to continue on their journey even when their route has been significantly altered.

Travel Well – Travel With Love – Travel With Wonder

And even though you may lose some special ones along the way, always travel with **_them_** in your heart, but please be aware, your *Journey is Subject To Change.*

Leo Stone

Facebook: @LeoStonePoetry
X/Twitter: @LeoStonePoetry
Email: leo@leostonepoetry.com
www.leostonepoetry.com

ACKNOWLEDGEMENTS

Every person who has appeared at some stage on my journey through this life, whether that be for the briefest of times as a bit-part, or as a co-traveller for some time, will all have helped me become the person I am.

I am far from perfect, and now fully understand that this is actually a totally unrealistic vision to be aiming for. I therefore acknowledge and appreciate your patience with me, it can't have been easy, I know…!

You can only be the person you are today, by having been the person you were yesterday.

The act of creating something, bringing something into being that had never existed before, is a truly wonderful thing. Creation in itself can only happen through, and is indeed the culmination of, a host of changes happening. This is why change is something that should not be feared. To get better at something, to learn something new, to be a better person, all takes change.

I continue to change, evolve and grow on a daily basis, some of these changes are so tiny that you hardly notice them, and some can be more obvious.

To those people who have helped me change, thank you, I am only who I am because of who you are.

Finally….

For the person thinking about buying this book, whether as a gift or for yourself, THANK YOU, I appreciate your consideration.

For the person who *did* buy this book to read it, or to gift it on, THANK YOU, I *really* appreciate your consideration.

For the person who isn't totally sure at this moment in time about anything, but was a little bit intrigued, THANK YOU, you will get to where you need to be, whether I join you on your journey for a little while or not, just take care of yourself.

For everyone who gets to this point, never forget, your
Journey is Subject To Change.

My Journey So Far

I was the youngest of four boys and we lived in a distinctly average three bed semi-detached. Mum and Dad worked hard to pay for everything that we needed, along with help from my Grandma.

Junior school came and went in a blink. At roughly the time when I went to secondary school, my older brothers one-by-one left home to start their own lives.

Secondary school was where I discovered that sport was my thing, education was not.

I stumbled into a job as a naïve sixteen year old and then, my first major BOOM!

My first proper day in the world of being an 'adult' - That horrible four letter word WORK.

Sorry, no, work wasn't the boom.

I fell head over heels in LOVE.

Inside ten minutes of walking through the front door on the very first day of starting my working life…….I KNOW….I kid you not….!!

But that's it, literally, both feet, hook, line and sinker.

The journey of my life had been altered beyond anything that had ever crossed my feeble young mind. I might not have recognized it like this at the time, but it had.

Then out of nowhere, no warning, nothing, my second major BOOM!

I lost a parent – my life was then thrown into yet more chaos, the like of which I had absolutely no comprehension of. My journey completely thrown off course again, but this time in a vastly different way to the first.

This is just life, doing what life does.

And everyone, without exception, has their own stories, everyone has their ups and downs as they journey through life.

And I wholeheartedly believe that Life *Is* A Journey And *Not* A Destination.

We will meet many other travellers as we all journey through this life. Some will come and go, and if you're really lucky some really important ones will join you on your onward journey.

We will also lose some of our nearest and dearest as we travel.

To shed a tear here and there, is the most normal and human of things to do, whether they be tears of sadness or total and utter joy.

We should never be ashamed of showing our emotions, they are the most honest communication that we can give.

There are times when we may need to hold them inside for a little while, but, when the time comes for them to be released.......then the time comes for them to be released.

That time has to be whenever time that is…..**Release** is the key component to keeping yourself healthy.

Taking time for reflection and thought is critical, it helps your inner balance to remain… balanced in a healthy and good way.

Rest, reflect, recharge, reset and go again……..

As you travel on your journey I wish you all the best and I hope that you can….

Travel Well – Travel With Love – Travel With Wonder

And even though you may lose some special ones along the way, always travel with **_them_** in your heart, but please be aware, your *Journey is Subject To Change.*

THIS SERVICE WILL CALL AT

Journey Subject To Change

Arriving At.1
Growing Up

Officially, I'm a grown up.

I know I certainly grew taller and bigger and acquired some sort of knowledge through this period, but really, me, a grown up?

Anyway….I was lucky enough for this to be a period of carefree play, with the biggest problems being the onset of teenage acne and the discovery of how much fun it was being lazy when it came to studying.

Note to self – Must try harder

The Blue Elephant

When I was very little
I mean a little babe in arms
I'm told that I was cute
I had some special charms

My Mum thought I was lovely
A competition just the thing
If I won, well you know
My praises they would sing

I know it sounds a little weird
Now looking back on it
But 'Bonny Baby' was the thing
And don't you know......Yes I was it....!

I won the competition
But I didn't have a clue
I told you I was little
I wasn't even two..!

That isn't quite the end of it
I won it twice you know
What happened next, a scandal
My third time was 'no-show'

I'm told it was fix
Some random rule I hear
My Mum she was advised…
'He's just too old my dear..!'

The third year we were pushing it
I'd just turned two for sure
Past my prime and aging
A 'baby' not no more

Journey Subject To Change

Still trauma didn't haunt me
Into tears I did not melt
Because I had an elephant
My Mum made in blue felt

Bath Night

I'm in the bath, it's Sunday night
I can hear them all outside
My brothers who are older
They've had their tea, I've cried

I'm too little, I'm no fun
I've got to have a bath
School tomorrow, once again
Must be clean for maths

Scrubbed, scraped, soaped and washed
Pyjamas, then to bed
Deep asleep in seconds
Not a thought within my head

I sleep a sleep so deep
No rousing me at all
I never even hear them
My brothers playing ball

Morning comes, house in chaos
Noise, lost socks, porridge
The cats hide from the riot
As outside the squirrels forage

Then stillness, silence, nothing
The hooligans released
Heading off to different schools
Education is the feast

Dad's at work already
His boss with orders hurling
Mum she left, as off we went
The plates she spins are whirling

Journey Subject To Change

But Sunday was the night
Just the one each week
A bath to get me clean
Then off to school I'd squeak

Gale Force Warning

The house it was a fortress
But I never thought it then
Surviving four young boys
Like a gale at force ten

Football, rugby, tennis
Golf and all the rest
Hide and seek, lacrosse
Yeah, at that we were the best

Clubs and bats and balls
Sticks and general carnage
Boisterous and rumbunctious
With energy unharnessed

The clever one, the sporty one
The one who can't decide
And then the little one who
Each Sunday night he cried

Spats and fights and falling out
They'd all tease and take the 'mick'
The little one, who'd always cry
Still, up for him they'd stick

The garden was just like the Somme
Grass if any, battered flat
With jumpers for some goalposts
And a stick used as a bat

The outside wall was painted
With a cross for target use
The four of us did run amok
We gave that house abuse

Journey Subject To Change

That house survived the worst we gave
We smashed a garden gnome
And even though we're all grown up
That house, it was our home

Freaky Looking Space Alien

The world it has revolved around too quickly I believe
Then again not quick enough, from puberty I need reprieve
I see that man has journeyed now into outer space
They've walked upon the moon, which is pock marked like my face

The zits, the spots, the craters, the flaming yellow blobs
Erupting on my face leaving murky looking globs
They tell me that I'm growing, sprouting up most everyday
But please can someone tell me, when this will go away?

Beneath these ghastly things that just cover all my face
Is stupid looking fluff, gathered where it can find space
I can't do 'nowt' about it, there's no way I can shave
I'd be be-heading blackheads and I'm simply not that brave

And then there is my voice, I dare not speak at all
It's scratchy then it's high, I think I've dropped a ball..!
The trousers I wore yesterday, now seem six inches short
Although slightly on the plus side, I'm better at my sport..!

I suddenly see muscles where before was only string
And I dare not even mention….my ding-a-ling-a-ling..!
I can throw the ball much further, I'm running faster too
My Mum just can't believe that I now need bigger shoes

Another thing that's happened, my mate who got a blister
I'm suddenly aware that he's got an older sister
We used to play Atari and footy here and there
Now at her boobs I can't resist I really have to stare

I've now been caught a dozen times, she looks me in the eye
And yes I feel embarrassed, but it's just teenage "I-Spy"…
I'm awkward and I'm sweaty, my hair is lank and greasy
Looking like I look, to get a girl's not easy

Journey Subject To Change

But for now I've got my sport, and that for me will do
As the way I look right now, I should be in a zoo
Everything is crazy, when what I need is 'Zen'
Said the boy who looks just like a freaky alien

Journey Subject To Change

'Oh!' Levels….

My exams they start tomorrow
I've not given them much thought
I've been busy doing other things
Lacrosse is *'life'* man - not just sport

Plus there's something else
It's really quite the thing
I'm captain of the team
I'd guess you'd call me 'King'

I've got to practice all the time
This ain't no part time gig
As re my future life
Oh yeah, lacrosse is really BIG

Lacrosse it is my future, but
Yeah I've heard the chatter
Exams I'm told are something
Mum and Dad say that they matter

But what on earth do they know?
It ain't like 'olden times'
There is this thing called 'Rap'
Where you make money from your rhymes

The world is changing fast
We could be 'nuked' tomorrow
Exams are just a pain
And to study causes sorrow

So there it is, that's the score
There's music, sport, lacrosse
It's a waste of time to study
Hey! Of my life I'm the boss

Journey Subject To Change

"Oh and Mum, I need your help…"
"There's a trip, the end of May"
"If I do the washing up"
"Can I say that you will pay?"

And that there is the rub
As in details there's a devil
To earn a decent future crust
I'll need more than one 'O' Level..!

Teenage Kicks

I think I must have blinked
There's no-one left but me
We were a house of six
And now there is just three

My brothers have all gone
When did they disappear?
There's Mum & Dad and me
And they always bend my ear

There are clothes upon the floor
In my bedroom, yes I know
And plates and cups and rubbish
Yes - It only seems to grow

Then there are my records
Oh yes, my pride and joy
I stick them on my turntable
And I'm a happy boy

Then I can't believe it..!
They're knocking on the ceiling..!
"That isn't music I can hear,
It's someone bloody screaming..!"

"Turn that racket down…!"
Is the next thing that they yell
But it's David 'Bloody' Bowie
'Oh come on, Bloody Hell..!'

Yeah, OK, that did it
I know I shouldn't swear
But this guy is so cool
I mean, just look at his hair

Journey Subject To Change

Dad chips in "You heard your Mum"
And I know I'm pushing it
'Yeah, OK, alright' I shout
Then mumble 'Bloody Shit..!'

And then there are the times
It's a liberty I'd say
I know they've been into my room
When I've been out all day

The clothes and plates and rubbish
Have been moved and it's all gone
I mean, that's my flippin' bedroom
They've been in, I think it's wrong

But just to keep the peace
I ignore it, keep it shtum
But I'll make 'em suffer for it
I'll be quiet and all glum

Mum says tea is ready
Like I'm bothered don't you know
But like the 'lovely boy' I am
My face I'd better show

Cheese and onion pie….again..!
This I can't believe
I told her I don't like it
It's like a sticky, yellow sneeze..!

It's this and nothing else
Oh yes, I know the deal
I'd prefer one of them curries
You know, a simple ready meal

Journey Subject To Change

So I'm eating and all quiet
You know, I'm acting glum
Then I get the soppy voice
"Are you ok? Tell your Mum"

I mumble deep into my pie
'I'm fine, yeah it's all grand'
"If you need to tell me something,
You know I'll understand."

I grunt and brush it off
I think 'Yeah right, like you were young!'
Then it's cake and chocolate sauce
I think 'My God, it looks like dung!'

Permission has been granted
For me to leave the table
I mean really what's the point
Would it make the world unstable?!

If I didn't ask permission
It would start a right old ruckus
And I knew the pie was cheap
Most certainly not pukka

I've escaped into the living room
And I've put the telly on
Thursday nights are ace
Top of The Pops, the latest songs

So that there is my life
I do sport, I don't do 'chicks'
All in all it's decent
And that's my teenage kicks

It's Difficult Being Different But…

I've got freckles everywhere.
I've a mole upon my neck.
My hair it's just all frizzy,
and I'm thinking 'What the heck…!'

My head is funny shaped.
Oh why can't I be normal?
I mean just in a natural way,
I don't mean smart and formal.

Then I've got some hair,
where it really shouldn't be.
My teeth are also crooked,
so please don't smile at me.

My nose it is quite pointy,
not sure what happened there.
And my ears are sticking out,
people seem to look and stare.

Please don't get me started,
on my arms and legs and body.
They have a mind all of their own,
to be honest they're quite shoddy.

My tummy is a little plump.
I've got a chunk or two.
Well yes, I'm underplaying it,
I'm like a hippo in a zoo..!

I see the 'Perfect People'.
I see them everywhere.
They're always looking at me,
from social media they stare.

Journey Subject To Change

They're all smiling and all pouty.
They're buff and tanned with shades.
They're jetting off to somewhere cool.
While I'm in Blackpool with my spade…

But I heard a little secret,
I think you'd like to know.
You know those 'Perfect People'?
The majority are 'faux'…!

I know it's really shocking,
but I'll tell you something else.
Behind the masquerade,
they're doing it for wealth..!

The things that they're posting,
like the vids and pics and stuff.
It's all for making money.
I mean that makes it all just 'guff!'

It isn't like my mates and me,
as the stuff we post is real.
Like the one where we're all crying,
when we ate our burger meal.

We were crying 'cos we laughed so hard,
it was just so super funny.
My mate put chips in his nose,
and hopped just like a bunny.

I know it sounds just super gross,
but you had to be just there.
Plus we'd got a mega-meal,
so those chips were going spare.

Journey Subject To Change

My mates are also different,
I guess they're just like me.
But they tell it like it is,
and that's the best way you can be.

We tell each other everything.
They're my besties, they're my 'crew'.
And yes sometimes we're narky,
but then we'll always talk it through.

So different, yeah, it's difficult,
or it can be here and there.
But with your mates beside you,
you've got someone who cares.

So difficult, it is a thing
that no-one can avoid.
But like I say, when you've got mates,
this life can be enjoyed.

The Job Awaits

My first day at work ever
Sixteen years old, totally clueless
I understood school
I understood sport
I understood hanging out with my mates
I did not understand the world
I certainly did not understand adults

I walk through a door I've never been through before
Little did I know…
How walking through a certain door at a certain time….
Can change your life…..

A high street bank, a decent job
For a lazy 16 year old
I go to the closest serving point
I look up to make eye contact
The person behind the screen looks up

Every single cell in my body tingles
My world as I know it has changed…….
With one look…….
Forever

I was scared as I walked in
Now……I'm totally and utterly dumbstruck
This thing, this is _**the**_ one thing….
I most certainly do not know anything about
Other than physics, I was pretty bad at physics

I know I've said my name and why I'm here
But now I'm just staring
My stomach was flipping anyway….
But now more than all the burger joints in the world combined

Journey Subject To Change

If there's a Guiness World Record for that, I've just claimed it
I'm also continually beating it with every passing second.

I feel the sweet, gentle, warm nectar of an angel being poured into
my ear, my brain which was short-circuiting with fear, has softly
descended into a stupor, the like of which is beyond any of the
alcoholic experiences I've had.
And there have been many which extend beyond sensible in the
extreme.
I realise this nectar is her voice telling where to go and sit.
Oh what bliss, I've been directed on this earthly plain by a
Goddess…!!

I am more than happy with my role of being her lapdog
My concept of the real world has evaporated
I see no-one, I'm aware of nothing
I'm senseless, numbed to the core
I drift on feet that are carried by tiny fluffy clouds
Subconsciously I'm aware of reaching my destination and turn to
sit…

I slump in utter despair on a ratty, dirty old chair
My world is bereft, I can no longer see 'My Goddess'
The pain of knowing that such beauty exists in the world
Yet here I am in this desert of isolation, chairs, doors, scratched
Perspex windows
My heart and soul weigh more than anything could possibly weigh,
they sink deeper and deeper as my desert turns to an icy wasteland.
The clouds at my feet have lifted above my head
They rain down an incessant, dirty, painful mix
Of stinging hail stones and bulbous rain drops filled with acid
Which soak through to my very skin after penetrating
My cheap and nasty suit which Mum thought looked nice

The years, decades, centuries of time drag on my skin
I feel the decay peeling the youthful skin from my flesh
My skin is left in place to hang down in bloody strips

The salt from the acid rain is rubbed deep into the open wounds
The skin is slowly scraped back into place
Using the sharp prongs of rusty filthy BBQ tool
The rancid particles of meat helping to seal the edges of the skin back in place
A world that had merely served as a schoolboys playground
Had, in a mere five minutes, swung from extremes I had never known
Heaven had cloaked me in an ethereal haze of heart thumping elation
Which evaporated faster than an elected politicians promises
Into a fetid swamp crawling with bloodsucking mosquitoes
From now on to be known as my co-workers and supervisors
Hell on Earth had truly been delivered in a box
Wrapped in the gangrenous entrails of a long dead unidentifiable creature

Fingernails scrape down the blackboard screaming in an incessant howl

I see the harpy standing in front of me……."This way please….."

The Job Awaits…….

Arriving At.2
Love

This word means so many different things to different people. These poems cover some (a very tiny part in all honesty) of my take on finding it, experiencing it, the joy of it, losing it, the fear of losing it, what it is and the power of it.

Love for me is the most powerful thing that exists.

This amuses me, as it is such an intangible thing, yet it touches everyone who has ever, and, will ever live. Whether that be through having or experiencing love, or even just the lack of it, no-one will ever be unaffected by love in one way shape or another.

I Didn't See

I didn't see this thing
I didn't see at all
I didn't think it possible
That I could be enthralled

But here it is, a thunderbolt
A sudden lightning strike
A thing of total power
Of which I had no sight

My life has changed forever
My path is not the same
What has brought this difference?
Does it even have a name?

Ah yes! The name is known to all
But some they still renounce
They liken it to prison
And away from it they flounce

Some they say that fools rush in
And some indeed they do
But can a thing so powerful
Be that easy to eschew?

Some they fear to feel the pain
That they've felt once before
Some they truly can't resist
They're always knocking at that door

Working hard to find it
Is not what you should do
When the time is right
This thing will come to you

Journey Subject To Change

This thunderbolt, this lightning strike
This thing from up above
This thing that changes lives forever
This thing you know is........LOVE

A Power Deep Inside

There's a power deep inside
The like of which is new
There's a power deep inside
And this power's linked to you

I've never felt this way before
And I cannot comprehend
When did this power start?
And could this power end?

My heart it seems to shiver
My heart it seems to shake
I fear that if you leave
My heart will surely break

How to keep this power going?
How to keep myself plugged in?
I know it's you I cannot lose
And us together's how I win

Figure out a way to keep
The power surging on
Figure out a way to make
Sure that you're never gone

I know exactly what to do
So I make a resolution
I resolve to keep forever
Finding a solution

A solution every day
That everyday I need to change
To alter what I need to
To keep you in my range

Journey Subject To Change

Reinvent, invigorate
Change and do not hide
I must always keep you close
To keep this power deep inside

It Could Be Today

Listen up my friend
I've something I must say
It won't take long, I promise
You'll soon be on your way

You hear all the songs
That tell of broken hearts
But please don't hide away
That isn't how love starts

Do not be afraid
Of what might lie ahead
And do not face the future
With thoughts all full of dread

Let each day arrive
Give it chance to be its best
You never know quite what may come
You might just be impressed

Do not overthink it
Let it be what it will be
You could look back in time
And be thankful, wait and see

So today I'm going to try
And let the world do what it will
Today could be the one
When you feel loves special thrill

Let yourself be open
To whatever ebb and flow
Let's just see what happens
You never really know

Journey Subject To Change

I'll let go of preconceptions
And with the breeze I'll sway
Because you really cannot tell
It could well be today

Dark Sky

If it wasn't for the dark sky
We couldn't see you shine
That's why my little star
I'm gonna make you mine

The many times I've spent alone
The nights I can't forget them
Those times they have a purpose
They help me see your spectrum

A starting point you have to have
For a journey to commence
There is a time and you will know
For getting off the fence

A starburst supernova
It split the sky asunder
I witnessed something magical
A thing of joy and wonder

My world of grey and drab
Then suddenly transformed
With colours of the rainbow
It now was all adorned

So dark skies have a purpose
Although they can feel harsh
Fun and joy and laughter
Can beneath them seem quite sparse

Hold your nerve and keep on going
The dark sky won't prevail
The reason that it's there at all
Is to see and grab the comet's tail…..

There's No One Thing

There's no one thing that makes things right
There's no one thing that suits all situations
There's no one thing that works whatever

There's no one size fits all
There's no one style that everyone likes
There's no one shape that always looks good

There's no pleasing all the people all the time
There's no point in worrying
There's no reason why it couldn't be you

There's always the chance it will work out
There's goodness all around if you can see it
There's always enough time if it means that much to you

There's No One Thing
There's No One
There's No
There's

There Is……..You

The Fable of The Boy and The Unknown Treasure

Please just take a moment, sit yourself down in a chair
I have a little tale to tell and with you I'd like to share

It won't take me very long and I hope that it won't drag
You never know you might enjoy, it could well be just your bag

Way back when it started, no, further back than that
A boy went on a journey with his trusty cat

Sorry no I've got that wrong, that's Dick Whittington
He had a cat and there were some rats, but that could be a pun

Let's start again but concentrate 'cos this time this is it
As we only have a little while to pause and chat and sit

A teenage boy ignorable, all awkward and unsure
He wasn't any looker but his heart was fairly pure

He entered the arena with nowt but teenage swagger
But let me state again for sure, he wasn't any Jagger

But here he was this spotty youth setting out upon his quest
He knew not where he headed but he knew he'd do his best

The problems really started from his first day on the road
He carried with him nothing much, then something changed the load

There were sorcerers out in the world he knew not of their spells
He was innocent in wicked ways, bedazzled by their hells

They painted pretty images that danced around his brain
The magic they'd implanted it was coupled with a pain

This thing that they'd created, the enchantment they had weaved
Was far stronger than a simple boy could ever have believed

Journey Subject To Change

His head it spun, his heart was heavy, in a way he'd never known
Little did he know this boy, but a secret seed was deeply sown

That night as he returned, to his camp and fellow folk
He spoke in tongues unknown to them, and of this thing he spoke

He raged, he flamed and he exulted in a way they'd never heard
His face grew red, his actions fierce, the way he was, was quite absurd

His kinfolk were enraptured though because they saw a change
One they were most pleased with, they knew this wasn't strange

It was like a rite of passage that we all must travel through
It had started in him early but more things would now ensue

They couldn't take the journey for him, it was his alone to travel
The mysteries that lay beyond, must be allowed to now unravel

The days they flashed across his brow and many folks he met
His path meandered here and there with no destination set

Some they seemed quite friendly and some just like a foe
He didn't know quite who to trust and along with whom to go

None of that did matter, this was his route to take
Sometimes you follow true, sometimes you're fooled by fake

Each passing day and chance encounter granted wisdom as he went
Each night he fell exhausted and dreamt within his tent

The colours in his dreams surpassed this earthly realm
The feelings that he felt, he thought would overwhelm

But each day he woke refreshed and ready for what came
And each night he had been altered, to never be the same

Journey Subject To Change

All of this was happening without his understanding
His heart took off from one place and in another it was landing

These changes manifested in the way he took each day
He never even feared all the demons that he slay

Tragedy unknown can hit, without a prior warning
And so it was this fateful day, as he got up that morning

Invited to a banquet with both food and drink a plenty
But little did he know that night, his world would soon be empty

The next day came, the news it broke, his King had died that night
He wasn't there, he didn't know, could he have fought the mighty fight?

The pain of having fought a battle is easier to take
Than to live not knowing if, you've made a huge mistake

Bereft and torn asunder with a pain too huge to bear
He railed against injustice and battled with despair

The wounds he had could not be seen, the pain was deep inside
He smiled each day upon his work and then each night he cried

He'd failed his King and Queen and had let his brothers down
Yet though he was the youngest he was handed down the crown

Through his trials and tribulations, through daily toil and test
The Queen now passed the crown to he, as he proved to be best

He had his faults and flaws, 'perfect' was not in danger
He'd proved that change to him though, was not a total stranger

So whilst there was a way to go the Queen had passed the mantle
Enamoured though his brethren weren't, they couldn't hold a candle

Journey Subject To Change

"Now I have to carry on" the junior King insisted
"But help is what I truly need and thus I must enlist it"

And once again his quest commenced after this hiatus
But no-one knew about the change in his regal status

He was viewed just as before, as foolish, young and rash
Yet little did they know, how their hopes he now would dash

The seed sown many months before by sorcerers most wise
Would now with wild abandon grow and grow to fill the skies

With the flower in abundance and a flame now re-ignited
The foes, the dragons and the demons now would all be smited

His power grew as more assured he strode into the future
His wounds they now were healing, guarded with a suture

He learned the ways of romance under guidance of his muse
The path they now would travel, together they would choose

But no-ones path is always smooth, as challenges will come
But one and one a two they make and that's a mighty sum

As two together moving forward they faced the world as one
Growing stronger day by day, as side by side they shone

The beguiling pretty images that had long ago been cast
Turned into something beautiful that would now forever last

The boy had now a man become and the treasure he could see
He hadn't known it at the time but a law now he'd decree

"I value just one thing in life and this will be my law
You and I forever, as non has ever been before"

Journey Subject To Change

"Death will come a-calling at some point for one and all
But support each other all the way and ne'er let either of us fall"

"Together is the only way to face the coming times
Only God can break asunder the things within my rhymes"

He spoke of many things throughout the years that came
The most frequent thing of which he spoke, it had a special name

The name is love and love is strong, the strongest thing of all
Whatever meets you on your way with love you will not fall

So unknown treasure may await you, as you travel on your way
You never know when it might strike as you move from day to day

Don't search with expectation, what will be will be
It will manifest itself, when the time is right for thee

It may be cloaked in unfamiliar, it may be something known
But be ever mindful, you never know when seeds are sown

And that my friend is all to say I hope you hear my word
Sometimes it's clear sometimes it's not, but do not be deterred

Tread your path from day to day and who knows what may come
The path may rise to meet your feet, you may feel the warmth of sun

Keep your hope and your resilience, deep within your chest
Be brave, be strong, be kind and always do your best

For one fine day, or rainy day, you never know quite which
Love may come a-calling and you'll feel a certain itch

A flame within your heart and soul that burns like none you've felt
Perhaps your heart you thought of steel might suddenly be smelt

Journey Subject To Change

And out will pour a love so strong that you will be entranced
I guarantee it's worth the risk, your life will be enhanced

Riches that you never knew, will be yours so hold them dear
Caress them softly, treat them kindly, be tender but be clear

There is no price or bounty that to this can justice do
Its value lies within the fact that this is just for you

It can only ever happen once and the price that you must tender
Is to give yourself completely and the whole of you surrender

But worry not about your path or what might lie ahead
As to worry is a useless thing, you'll live your life in dread

Instead relax and breathe, and commit to being kind
And you my friend, an unknown treasure, one day will truly find

A Heart On Fire

There is no red box on the wall
There is no glass for you to break
There is no button which to press
There's no escape route you can take

There's no detector on the ceiling
There's no alarm point near the door
There's no large bell for you to ring
There's no firemen to call

A fire drill cannot be learned
A fire drill is of no use
A fire drill will not save you
As the fire's running loose

The flames can't be extinguished
The flames cannot be seen
The flames won't cause you harm
But they set fire to your dreams

There is no fire blanket
There is no bucket filled with sand
There is however someone
Who will always hold your hand

So how can this be fire
When flames I cannot see?
So how can this be good
When a fire's bad for me?

I surrender to its power
I surrender to the heat
I surrender finally
As I know this can't be beat

Journey Subject To Change

My dreams are burning brightly
My dreams fill with desire
My dreams are you and me
As for 'You' my heart's on fire

Journey Subject To Change

All The Way

The sun it shines so brightly
The moon reflects upon the lake
But a marriage strong and good as ours
Only you and I could make

There are times when we'll be happy
There are times when we'll be sad
But as long as we're together
My heart will be so glad

Each morning as I see your face
I once again realise
I have in life a special one
The greatest sort of prize

Each moment that I spend with you
Is one I can't replace
Everything in life, that I could want
Is there within your face

The times we are together
Each second, every day
It goes deeper in my soul
That I love you all the way

A Love Told In Film

Against All Odds we fell in love
Thank God and stars above
Risky Business though it is
We shared a special magic kiss

Our lives were joined through *Sliding Doors*
What's yours is mine, what's mine is yours
Involved with *Serendipity*, it did what fatum does
It made us feel a special kind of truly magic buzz

Stardust had been sprinkled and the stars they had aligned
The Gods agreed this was indeed, a very special find
They said it would be right enough to be a *Wonderful Life*
And yes indeed it was decreed that we'd be man and wife

Up there in the heavens and not in *Notting Hill*
They decided that our lives with love, they now would truly fill
It's Complicated though, sometimes within this world
Each other's arms is the place where we should stay all tightly curled

We could get *Sleepless in Seattle*, or go and *Meet Joe Black*
But together here at home, we should always hurry back
So through life's rough and tumble, like *Marley & yes Me*
Never let the both of us, forget *Love Actually*

An Officer and A Gentleman, I always try to be
And a *Pretty Woman* is, what you'll always be to me
And whilst *Paying It Forward*, don't overcook our goose
We always must remember, it began with old *Footloose*

Jackpot

I lie quite still and silent and listen to you breathe
It's something truly wonderful I struggle to believe

How I, who is not worthy, ends up lying by your side
It's something truly magical, that cannot be denied

Somewhere within my past, when I didn't hesitate
I rolled the dice and played the cards and somehow it was fate

You and I together was the jackpot in the game
My life from that day on would never be the same

It's in the quiet times when the world is all asleep
The magnitude of things gone past into my mind they creep

I come back to the present and I'm trying not to move
As if somehow me keeping still again my love does prove

But this sacrifice of mine, whilst miniscule I know
To you my sleeping beauty, again my love does show

I know you're not aware of this story in the dark
Even though you are the one who added kindle to the spark

There you go that's all there is, a simple thing to do
Me lying quiet in the dark, another ode to you

It Isn't And It Is

Love it is the whisper
That roars within your heart
Love it is the end
Where your life begins to start

Love it isn't anything
But everything there is
Love it is the champagne
With that extra special fizz

Love it doesn't rule you
It governs every choice
Love it is that silence
Where you really have a voice

Love it makes you fly
With your feet upon on the floor
Love makes you a beggar
When you've never been worth more

Love it shows you everything
But there's nothing that you want
Love it makes you thirsty
As it flows from every font

Love is not demanding
Whilst devouring your soul
Love is not a sport
Yet somehow your only goal

Love it knows your everything
Whilst leaving you quite dumb
Love it makes you feel alive
And yet beautifully quite numb

Journey Subject To Change

Love is not a membership
Where there is a fee to pay
Love it is commitment
That you honour everyday

Love it asks you questions
Whilst giving you the knowledge
Love teaches you everything
You cannot learn in college

Love is for the brave
Who enter with faint heart
Love is for the nervous
Who don't know where to start

Love is not for everyone
Yet everyone's invited
Love it is the pain
That will make you feel delighted

Love it will arrive
When the time is right
Love it can depart
In the middle of the night

Love it costs you everything
But no money is required
Love it is the jackpot
When your ticket has expired

Love needs no explanation
But it never quite makes sense
Love helps you make decisions
When you've sat upon the fence

Journey Subject To Change

Love is warm and fiery hot
Whilst giving you a chill
Love takes away your words
As you write with Shakespeare's quill

Love is fluid, always changing
But solid like a rock
Love is years a-flashing by
Like seconds on a clock

Love is not what you expect
But everything you need
Love is moving very slowly
As you race at break-neck speed

Love is always round the corner
But not where you expected
Love is fun and joy and wonder
As the more you are infected

Love is not a destination
But it helps you as you travel
Love keeps it altogether
When your life seems to unravel

Love can't stop things from happening
But it helps to get you through
Love can help you when you're one
But it's better as a two

Love is everything you didn't see
But it's everything you feel
Love seems just like a dream
Yet it makes it all so real

Journey Subject To Change

Love is always out of reach
If you try to chase it down
Love is never ever funny
If it makes you look a clown

Love is in your darkest hour
It illuminates you there
Love exacerbates the pain
As you're going through despair

Love is giving and forgiving
As you receive and you forgive
Love it forms the strongest bond
You'll encounter as you live

Love requires an open heart
To shut out all, but your one love
Love is being kind and gentle
When push, it comes to shove

Love it is quite simple
But exceptionally complex
Love it will obey
As you, it then directs

Love wants nothing much
But all you have to give
Love my dear is you
And that's all I need to live

Journey Subject To Change

Abandoned Fruit

Confusion reigns within my mind
Am I cruel or am I kind?

Do I do the things that please you?
I hug and hold, caress and squeeze you

I whisper words straight from my heart
But that is when the troubles start

I want too much, I pressurize
I see the tears form in your eyes

The floods they come, the valley drenched
From your heart I've now been wrenched

I'm tossed aside, I'm cast away
To return again? Who can say

I'm crushed inside, I fall apart
There is no joy within my heart

A heart once loved is now destroyed
A thing so full is now devoid

I slink away, my heart will rust
Once alive, I turn to dust

I'll hide within my corner bleak
Of love and joy I will not speak

So once a lover, soulmate, friend
It brings me to this sorry end

Abandoned fruit upon the vine
To shrink and shrivel not to wine

Journey Subject To Change

You were here and so was I
The mighty odds we would defy

But now all's left for me to say
Is how I truly rue the day…..

Journey Subject To Change

Love Dreams of a Future

Today I was mistaken, I thought I stood a chance
My future looked all rosy, all full of song and dance
Then off it went, my future, it swirled around the drain
"We've lost her" were the words that flooded round my brain

Love letters we had written and plans they had been made
Into the ground they'll now all go, to be covered by a spade
For life it had a different plan, which with me it didn't share
It's like you know this life, it doesn't really care

Another life has gone, snuffed out just like a flame
My world it has been shattered to never be the same
But why do these things happen, why does hate exist at all
I just want to hide away forever, in a deep dark cave I'll crawl

But then again I rally and declare an oath so strong
I'll get up every day and I'll make them hear my song
Yes the world is tough and life it can be hard
But by fighting everyday you can play a different card

So I'll face the world so cold with a heart so big and strong
Cuz in my life you'll always be, as that's where you belong
I'll go out and fly a banner and declare my love to you
I'll show the world love's winning and it cannot keep us blue

For love it is the one great power the only thing supreme
It is the greatest power that will always make us dream
To dream of things that might yet be, of things all bright and new
To dreams of love through day and night, a dream of me and you

Stupid

I lay upon our bed last night, I felt the empty space
I closed my eyes, the tears they came, I visualized your face

I'm not sure what really happened, it just sort of passed me by
I'm lying here without you now and my eyes begin to cry

Yesterday was perfect, all our days were full and sweet
I saw my life before me, my future felt complete

That's when the freight train hit me, that's when my world blew up
I missed the signs, ignored the truth & dropped the loving cup

I'd drank my fill of happiness and grew giddy with its taste
But I grew lazy, let it slip and precious things were laid to waste

I didn't take the time, to keep the magic real
I forgot to let you know, how good you made me feel

Simple, it was simple, just pay attention, take some care
A thought, a touch, a gentle word, just be present, just be there

But no I couldn't do it, I just didn't take the time
I lost your love, I let you down, now you're no longer mine

My days are cold and empty, my nights they are so hollow
So pain, regret and fear and anguish, are mine in which to wallow

So please believe my pleas, as I go under one last time
My stupidity has granted me, a life sentence for this crime

Stupid, stupid, stupid, such a simple word to say
But that is what I am, to have lost your love this way

A Shattered Heart

A billion, trillion pieces, all shattered on the floor
My heart had never broken in such a way before

The tiniest of fragments all scattered on the ground
I try to pick them one by one, not all of them I found

I tried to put them back together as I've done so in the past
But as some parts are missing, feeling whole just doesn't last

For fleeting moments here and there, I think everything's alright
But when I look inside my heart, I see the darkness of the night

Darkness isn't shy you know, it's happy to be seen
It loves to have the spotlight, for its brazen and obscene

It dances in an evil jig, its hands go everywhere
I'm looking for the light, but all I see there is despair

It's greasy and it's horrid and it sticks so on your skin
So fun and smiles and happy times just cannot begin

The vile and putrid stench, of this stinking wretched curse
Puts a vacuum all around your joy, and makes the world seem worse

This is how it feels, now my universe has crumbled
It's like a horror movie into which my life has stumbled

But there isn't a director sitting calmly shouting 'cut'
The dogs from hell are running free and chewing on my foot

They've eaten all the juicy parts, the bits that contained joy
Snaffled up and gobbled down, just like a saveloy

I'm left now with the offal, the bits that no-one wants
People stop and stare at me like I'm a dirty 'nonce'

Journey Subject To Change

I know this isn't real but it sure as hell seems true
It's like the world and everyone can see I'm not with you

Inside I feel like people, are judging by their looks
They make a note of time and place and write it in their books

If something is reported like a crime or some wrongdoing
It's me that they'll be looking for, and a barrister start suing

For this is what you've done to me, by exiting stage left
My life is wholly empty, I'm destroyed, I'm just bereft

My heart it stands quite proudly, a-top the vampires stake
My eyes and all my innards the buzzards now can take

I'm left to rot and crumble and decay all on the floor
Step over me, avoid this plague, it's me you must abhor

I am no longer worthy to be thought of as alive
Erase me from your memories in order to survive

So crumble me beneath your feet just like a baby's rusk
All thoughts of me will fade away like day into the dusk

By fall of night I'm fully gone, I never did exist
My name will disappear from off your birthday list

It's like an amputation but for you without the pain
My life will slowly seep away like sewage down a drain

Your world it will return to something shiny and brand new
And if you ever think of me, it's like I'm something on your shoe

We've gone our separate ways you said it's for the best
And six feet underground is where I'll take my final rest

Arriving At.3
Death

A very short section for good reason.

Death, weirdly, is the thing above all others, which means we should always try and extract the very best that we can out of this journey we're all on. We shouldn't ignore it (death), but neither should we let it cloud over the wondrous joy that is 'life'.

No matter what we do, certainly at this particular point in time (I mean in relation to scientific advancement and so on), it will always be there for us (and our loved ones), whenever that may be, so we should concentrate on 'living life' as best as we can.

We should always be mindful it is there and talk about it when we need to, but this thing, death, is the reason why life is so fragile, precious and beautiful.

Death is Not The Problem

Death is not the problem,
it's life that causes grief,
because you know this life,
it's too damn short and brief.

Death we know is certain,
life we know is not,
don't be wasting all your time,
on counting what you've got.

Death should be ignored,
in life as much as possible,
because my friend you know,
that death is just not stoppable.

Death is not the prize,
for winning at life's quiz.
Death is just a thing,
it is just what it is.

Death should not be feared,
life's too good to waste on that,
be happy in your life,
before they lie you flat.

Death arrives when it arrives,
when life it has to go,
so give it all you've got,
in rain, or sun, or snow.

Death is there just waiting,
like the sky is there above,
life is truly special,
so fill it full of love.

Journey Subject To Change

Death is not the problem,
yes, it's too damn short and brief,
but live your life with love,
as 'time' it is the thief.

I Know This Much Is True

There's this thing that I'm aware of
I notice more each day
You're just getting on with life
And I really have to say

The time it seems to fly by
I started working yesterday
But I look upon the calendar
That's now eight months away

I remember on my first day
It really was a doozy
I met this stunning woman
Her name I know is Susie

That night when I got home
From my first day at the job
I told my Mum and Dad
That this girl my heart did rob

This thing to me's a mystery
I mean romance, love and stuff
Cos I'm a rough and tumble guy
Girls and kissing was just guff

Then, that first day happened
It is seared in my brain
And I see her everyday
I'll just never be the same

And then this unexpected thing
It hit me in the head
From absolutely nowhere
My Dad he just dropped dead

Journey Subject To Change

It's a night I can't remember
It's a night I won't forget
I had stayed out at my mates
It's a night full of regret

I couldn't know the future
It came out of the blue
His heart it stopped that night
And there's nothing I could do

I'd lost my Granddad years ago
But then I was just little
This was truly massive
As I found my heart was brittle

My Dad was gone so suddenly
I didn't have a chance
I was still a troubled teen
So he hardly got a glance

I didn't spend the time I should
To sit and chat with him
Life was fun and to be lived
I did most things on a whim

But you have to truly face it
There's nothing you can do
There's no-one else within the world
Who can live that time for you

There's not much I remember
Of the time right after this
It has melded into nothingness
But him I truly miss

Journey Subject To Change

It taught me time is precious
The most precious gift of all
How my Mum survived it
I just couldn't really call

So if you have a loved one
Who means the world to you
Tell them now, don't waste your time
As I know this much is true…..

When they're gone, they're gone
And there's nothing you can do

Photographic Memory

I see my Dad he's holding me
A babe in blanket white
Then a toddler in something blue
My God I look a sight

Then on a beach with Grandad
My Mum she called him 'Pop'
He's wearing shades and looking cool
With a style that looks quite 'top'

Then 'arty' shots whilst still a kid
I look like butter wouldn't melt
And I loved my little elephant
The one made of blue felt

Pictures then on holiday
I know just where in Wales
In clothes that very probably
Were purchased in the sales

Junior school, green uniform
Chubby cheeks and tie askew
I was brought up so polite
Saying 'Please' and 'Yes, thank you'

In the garden with my Mum
We had kittens don't you know
Flag and Fluffa, Casper too
But two they had to go

Fluffa was the one we kept
I really loved that cat
Then we had a rabbit
It sadly ended flat..!

Journey Subject To Change

My Dad like Frank Sinatra
My Mum like Doris Day
I wish I had more pictures
I miss them everyday

When A Feather Comes To Visit

I was out in the garden sorting out weeds
Then after that, I thought I'd plant seeds
The day was all pleasant not too cold or too hot
The right sort of day to sort out your plot

Then I drifted away as a butterfly passed
My hands they grew still as I dwelt on the past
My brother arrived to just say 'Hello'
Which is strange as he passed some time ago

But the feather it floated down from above
It's him a-come visiting, sending me love
That's what I think, that is my choice
Oh how I wish I could still hear his voice

My eyes with liquid in corners do fill
One or two more and I'm sure they will spill
But not on this day, 'cos the feeling is good
It's nice to remember the old 'brotherhood'

I think of him often, most every day
I think of our talks and what he would say
The passage of time can help with the healing
My heart fills with warmth which is such a nice feeling

So 'Thanks for the visit' I think in my head
Don't stand on the seeds, watch where you tread
When the seeds have all grown and started to bloom
I'll find you right there, in my heart you've got room

So 'Thanks once again' I think and move on
I've got to continue but he's never all gone
He was never the one in feelings to smother
But he was OK…..Yes…….I love my big brother…..

Arriving At.4
Starting A Family

A prime example of life throwing in a curve ball, resulting in a major turning point in the journey of my life.

There are some things in life that just cannot be explained. Science or no science, some things can just happen, or not, for no obvious reason whatsoever.

You're on auto-pilot, you're busy, you're living life.

You work hard to earn enough money to do all the 'adulting' stuff you're supposed to, then this thing that should be the next step on your path of life is………..missing.

What are you supposed to do?

Talk…………..that's the best answer, talk about it.

You have to work through these things, you have to face them and deal with them, avoidance will do you no good.

The best way to deal with this sort of thing is to truly open your heart and talk about it. There is only one way you can find your way *through* to the other side of something that looks totally insurmountable, talk it through.

It may not be easy, it may not remove the pain, but it will help you survive and move forward with a shared understanding of what your '*new*' future can look like.

Embryonic

You know when you wake up in the middle of a dream?
I've suddenly appeared and I don't know where I've been
But I feel quite warm and lovely as I lie within my ocean
I'm exactly where I'm meant to be, I'm peaceful here just floatin'

I haven't any concept of what any of this means
I haven't any concept but it feels like it's dreams
Something truly magical would appear to be in play
Something truly magical is what I hear somebody say

There isn't an agenda, well, not one of which I've knowledge
I've a feeling that I've lots to learn but not necessarily in college
I also have this feeling, it's sort of there without me knowing
That for some rhyme or reason I'm supposed to be like.......
growing....?

I just don't really know what any of this means
I hear talk about a beanstalk and some magic beans
If I knew what they were, it might just make more sense
But something major's happening, something quite immense

It appears that there's a journey, that somehow I am on
I don't where it started and I don't know for how long
There's laughter, joy and happiness and talk of no protection
I'll leave that to another time as of that I've no conception

As I bob within my world, of fluid warmth and safety
I'm going on this journey and I'll go where it does take me
For now I will not bother, as tired is what I'm growing
I hear a bunch of voices talk of seeds that have been sowing

It doesn't make a lot of sense, I'm here where 'ere that be
I have a sense of being, I have a sense of 'me'?
I hear another voice saying 'blooming' saying 'rosy'
I think I'll leave that where it is as now I'm feeling dozy

Journey Subject To Change

I start to drift away from thoughts
I start to drift away
I start to drift away
I wish that I could stay………

IVF - The Excitement - (Part 1 of 4 Part Piece)

For months you have been prodded, poked and then inspected
And then repeatedly, repeatedly, repeatedly injected
But this is what it takes, it's the sacrifice you make
You cannot make a cake if some eggs you do not break

Then there's been the samples that both of you provide
All the time you're doing this you're by each others side
The feeling of self-conscious is where the journey starts
But progress down the road a bit and that feeling soon departs

Both of you just know that this is how it's done
It'd feel a little nicer if somehow it was more fun
You knew a challenge it would be, so be it, bring it on
The two of you will make it through as together you are one

Destinations beautiful, down tough roads is how they're reached
The both of you are hoping that your project won't be beached
Then comes a certain day, the timing all seems good
Your body full of hormones, it is now all a-flood

You're feeling bruised and battered, but somehow make it through
Now there's simply nothing more the two of you can do
Be patient and be calm and live your life as normal
Try to be observant, but try not to be too formal

A few weeks down the line a nervous day awaits
Oh the waiting and the fretting, the tension it creates
Scans and beeps and conversations, yet again inspected
Could it be the thing, that we never had expected?

You're walking down a corridor, thinking "Wow" and "What the heck!"
You have a glow the two of you like you've eaten "Ready Brek"
There's a secret that you carry, somewhere hidden deep inside
And you hope it isn't obvious how recently you've cried

The feeling is so weird, it's not one you've had before
You can't wait to be alone and get through your front door
You shut the door and cry again, they're tears of joy that night
'The Excitement' it envelops you and you hold each other tight

IVF - The Suspicion - (Part 2 of 4 Part Piece)

The weeks have passed like treacle
That's been stored in freezer tanks
It's been the weirdest thing
But you know you must give thanks

You've been mindful and observant
And tried not to be too formal
But there's a silent thing unsaid
Something feels not normal

A few days in a caravan
North Wales don't you know
It wasn't too exotic
As holidays they go

You took it slow and easy
No rushing here and there
But somehow something happened
And you both just feel the scare

There isn't much that's said out loud
But there's something just like fission
Strange is how you're feeling
You both know 'The Suspicion'

IVF - The Sentencing - (Part 3 of 4 Part Piece)

You knew you would be coming back
But this visit's slightly early
You try to be lighthearted
But you somehow feel quite surly

Scans and beeps are nothing new
Always they were expected
But sighs and getting colleagues
Has now got your minds infected

The thing that neither of you said
Might just be coming true
Two professionals now look
Saying "Bad news we've got for you…"

As they leave you for a moment
He puts his arm around your shoulders
The both of you are shaking
Now his tears they fall like boulders

His knees begin to crumble
The floor comes up to meet him
For you he must be strong
This thing cannot defeat him

His soul, his head, his heart
Are vacuums, they're devoid
But this will be the something
That you just cannot avoid

They say about what happens next
It washes through your head
This is what you have to face
'The Sentencing' you dread

IVF - The Decision: Life 2.0 - (Part 4 of 4 Part Piece)

You're young and you are healthy
But these things they matter not
Because the thing that matters most
Is the one thing you've not got

There's no specific reason
There's nothing to be found
They've tested virtually everything
You both seem fairly sound

The treatment plan has finished
There's nothing more to offer
For where you live determines
The money in the coffer

Alternatives there are
If you wish to look that way
They give you all the options
But yours it is the final say

You've considered all the choices
You've talked most days and nights
You've thought it through quite thoroughly
You think you've got it right

There was a version of your life
You hoped how it might go
But this is 'The Decision'
It's Life, but 'two-point-oh'

I'll Carry You And You Carry Me

I do not know the science and I cannot find the words
When your hopes are crushed to crumbs just to feed the birds

When the plan for your life was ripped into shreds
As the doctor said the words that you dread

You think about life and all that you've done
You think of your hopes and what they've become

Have I really been bad? Do I deserve this?
Is the devil just there? Did I hear him hiss?

In the pain of the moment nothing makes sense
Your heart's bleeding out, it has no defence

The two of us started all full of hope
Now our lives seem to hang at the end of a rope

It just cannot be, the doctor has said
Is it wrong now to think that I wish I was dead?

But there's more than just me in this plan to consider
It's time to be strong we're in this together

You think of yourself and how you have failed her
But this is the time to act like her saviour

Now is the time when love really counts
When they need you there, they must feel every ounce

They truly must know how much that they mean
You're way past the point of keeping them keen

You're all fully in, both feet to your neck
Even though joy just looks like a speck

Journey Subject To Change

They say time's a healer, but you don't want to hear
It's hard to accept when you can't stop the tears

The doctor was kind she'd done this before
But your strength it seeped out, all over the floor

There isn't a choice, there's no coming back
You feel like a failure for all that you lack

There's no-one on earth who can understand this
But you know that's a lie as you feel their kiss

You must carry on, you know this is so
With the love that you share you'll give it a go

I'll carry you and you'll carry me
What lies in the future we'll just have to see

You Carry Me And I'll Carry You

They say that a void will never be gone
But to vanquish a void you have to stay strong

You still have this thing that no others possess
The pain that you've suffered you may yet redress

A vacuum was formed that sucked in your dreams
Your life fell apart as it ripped at the seams

But there in the dark with the pain and the hurt
There still was this thing, that would not desert

Right under the surface, deep down in the core
Love was still strong where the feelings were raw

The love that was formed right at the beginning
Would always ensure that the pain was not winning

There once was a void and a vacuum was there
But into the dark we no longer stare

A void and a vacuum can only exist
If the love that you share does not persist

To vanish a vacuum, to vanquish a void
Your love must stray strong it can't be destroyed

We'll all suffer pain and heartache and loss
But never forget, that your love is the boss

Love is the thing that will help you stand tall
Even when you've got your backs to the wall

But you carry me and I'll carry you
Together with love we're sure to get through

Never Here But Always There

Twenty three is what you'd be, if the journey had been smooth
But that's the thing when living life, some things you do not choose

The film inside my head, in which you sing and dance
That is one we didn't make, we didn't get that chance

There's many more all on repeat, that go throughout the years
But that's the thing that no-one sees, they all end up in tears

The one lay on the carpet where you gurgle like a drain
I laugh until I realise, it's not true and then it's pain

Daddy's girl for a little while, I would carry you on high
The fantasy again it fades and once again I cry

A sunny day, a butterfly, you try to catch in vain
You giggle, smile and burp and again here comes the pain

The time you fought to wear a skirt that frankly was a belt
I get cross but Mum stays cool, and both of you my heart you melt

You and Mum your bond so strong, two girls against poor me
This is a scene that never was, something I'll never see

Then boys arrive and Oh My God, I live in constant fear
But I needn't worry, it's not real and it's gone with just a tear

You find the one, my heart is broken, is he good enough?
I resolve to be so brave, for you I must be tough

If that boy he crosses you, he'll have hell to pay
I make it clear for him to see that he will rue the day

But all is good, he treats you right, I vaguely warm to him
Yet in my mind I must recall that this is just a 'sim'

Journey Subject To Change

It don't exist, it never was and it can never be
But you my darling daughter will always be with me

So here we go, it's wedding day, oh hell I'm going to cry
But these are tears of happiness, my heart for you does fly

I hold onto your Mum and I bless the luck we've had
But dreams just aren't reality, they always turn out bad

My precious girl I tell you, I won't give away the bride
I'll lend you to your husband, but I'm always at your side

My speech you know is epic, it gets groans and it gets cheers
And this I guarantee you, someone ends in floods of tears

Oh yes that's me it isn't you, because we never got this day
I never danced with both my girls, our song they didn't play

It's when my darling daughter, I see you with your Mum
I can just imagine, all that you've become

But that isn't what was meant for us, for your Mum and me
You were never here, but always there you'll be

Arriving At.5
Daft

Being daft and not always being serious is an absolute essential, just like a buffet car on a long train ride, it helps to get you through.

You may have to choose the right moments, a serious job interview….maybe not, but there will be times when it's better to be able to cry with laughter, than just cry because that's how you're feeling.

This is one of the stops on the journey that some people will choose to skip by selecting the more 'direct' route….I would advise against this and wholeheartedly recommend calling in here.

**Note to Reader – This is one stop where you have a genuine active choice over pausing your journey here intermittently. There is also an option for those travelling by car to visit here, for those on that method of transport, this will be signposted – "Relief Road".

Journey Subject To Change

If Only……

If only doesn't work you know
I know because I've tried
It really is a feeble thing
To try and save our pride

If only……
I'd had teachers who could actually do their job

If only……
My first boss had not been such a snob

If only……
All my colleagues had worked as hard as me

If only……
They could see how good that I could be

If only……
They had bothered, I would have stuck around

If only……
They had listened, my ideas they were sound

If only……
Is an excuse to cover your own tracks

If only……
Is a way to hide away from truthful facts

If only……
Is a thing to make some things feel better

If only……
Is a trick not used by a 'go-getter'

Journey Subject To Change

If only……
Can work wonders, when your ego has been hurt

If only……
Eases pain, when your confidence deserts

If only……
I had spent some proper care and time
Then maybe I could finish this really awkward rhyme……!!

How To Be Average

No-one talks of average, or being little and ignored
No-one talks of bumbling along, and being vaguely bored

These are things that matter though, they're the things I understand
These are things that I relate to, this is me, it is my land

Yes I'm sure it's rather lovely to be a superstar
To have more money than you need, to have a private bar

To be the leader of a team or to be the boss at work
Someone who looks important, who's never been a jerk

Someone whose always featured on the cover of a mag
But I have to be quite honest, it sounds just like a drag

Like every child's a champion or everyone's a winner
Your talking crap it's not like that, like I forget me dinner

I'm just not that together, I'm not all smiles and cheers
Out of bed and dressed, now that calls for some beers

I think I'm just low maintenance and there's nothing wrong with that
I managed school, or just about, an exam or two I sat

Results they weren't forthcoming, I just didn't work that hard
I was young and I enjoyed myself, playing footy in the yard

I haven't got a massive car or a house that's big and posh
But I'm healthy and I'm happy and I have a daily wash

I don't fly around the world and stay in fancy places
But I smile at all I meet and I see their happy faces

The riches I have got, are being decent, kind and caring
And I'm alright, it's going well, my friends care how I'm faring

Journey Subject To Change

I have a love, a special one, who I love with all my heart
They love me cos of who I am and not because I'm smart

I'm careful with me money, I don't go spending daft
I'll buy it if I need it, but not on overdraft

I've a roof above my head, I've warm clothes upon my back
I've food within my fridge, for essentials I don't lack

What I've got I've paid for and I've everything I need
Yeah I'd like a little more but I wouldn't call it greed

But in this thing called life, there's a fine line to be tread
To do the things you want and need and all before you're dead

You're never sure of when that is, so you go all hell for leather
Then things all change and that's not right, it's now all hell for
pleather

Either way the real thing is to get yourself some balance
Spend a little, save a little, I know it's quite a challenge

Cut yourself a little slack 'cos no-one knows it all
Sometimes it's right, sometimes it's not, sometimes it's tough to call

One thing I know above all else, is life's not competition
It won't make us any happier if we feel we're on some mission

It's a journey we must travel, it's not about the destination
It's a train on which we ride but we know not which our station

Recline within your seat it's the only one you've got
And wherever you maybe, be sure that it's your spot

You're where you are just meant to be, right at this current time
You were meant to be right here, indulging in this rhyme

Journey Subject To Change

So where next upon your journey, I don't know I must confess
But that's the thing for everyone, it's just a mangled mess

But that's OK believe me, we're not all perfect here
Make it up as you go along, just play it all by ear

When all is said done, there's less done more than said
And there are days I must admit, when I wished I'd stayed in bed

But this is it your journey, you're well upon your way
Go on, get up and smile, you might enjoy today

We cannot all be heroes and we all can't be some star
A little further down the road but we cannot know how far

Beyonce I am not, nor am I Taylor Swift
Do I even have a talent or some special hidden gift?

I tell you what I have got, I haven't got a clue
But here I am still trying and for me that just will do

Intentions, Distractions and Multiply Fractions

I know I put them in here right at the very start
But now I just can't see them, silly daft old fart
I tucked them in all safe and sound and snug
Then some old silly bugger, he got hold of the rug

With a short solid snap, they pulled that rug hard
Now I'm on Google looking at chard
How did that happen? I haven't a clue
Ooh look at that, blue coloured glue…!

Me get distracted?….That rarely does happen
Once I get going, I get quite a crack on
Typing away, all focus and poise
Never distracted by…..oooh what's that noise..!?

Anyway, quick, right back to the plot
Oh damn, my coffee's no longer hot
Down to the kitchen, I'll microwave that
Oh look outside, there's that lovely cute cat

Press all the buttons, the cup's gone inside
I'll look at the paper while it's having its ride
Quizzes and tests, that'll get the brain going
Multiply fractions..! The brains to-and-fro-ing

What was that 'ping' I heard in the kitchen?
Oh damn now it's started, my eyes flippin' twitchin'
I think I'll have coffee, I could do with a drink
Why's all that washing still in the sink?

I'd best get it done, while I'm here and all focus
Oooh look in the garden, I'm sure that's a crocus
I'll flick on the radio…..I've had many mentions
But first while I think, I'd best set intentions

Journey Subject To Change

You see that's just me, my head's on the go
But once I get started I'm just in the flow
I'm sure that I've written them down once before
Was that my intentions sneaking out of the door....?

Know It All

We're not meant to know it all and that I know for sure…..

There are some who know an awful lot
And clever stuff you know

There are some who know a little
But they're happy as they go

There are some there in the middle
Who know a fair amount

There are some for unknown reasons
Who think their thoughts don't count

I'm really not too sure
Who decides just who is clever

I guess it must be someone
Perhaps his name is Trevor?

Does it really matter?
I'm really not too sure

But one thing is for certain
It's not me who's keeping score

Some they use all fancy words
Like mellifluous, imbue

Some are good with numbers
I mean more than two plus two

Some are good at art
They like to paint and make and write

Journey Subject To Change

Some are good at sport
They can kick a ball just right

This brings me to the end
Of this thing that I have thought

This brings me to the end
So I'll keep the ending short

No-one knows it all
As I said right at the start

But the one thing I am sure of
Is we all know how to fart

The Master Burglar

Confidence, strength and self-belief
They were the things that were stole by the thief
The culprit appears a master of stealth
As it also appears he's nabbing my health..!

He creeps in-between the strands of daylight
He makes not a sound, to cause not a fright
He's furtive and quiet and he's never been seen
There's no finger prints, he's incredibly clean

He snaffles at will without making a sound
And when you look up he can never be found
I glanced in the mirror as a movement I saw
But when I looked up he'd snook out the door

It appears that he knows me and where I will be
I think it must happen when I'm having my tea
I don't realise till the very next day
That yet one more thing he's stolen away

I'd have called Scotland Yard or the local police
But that's one more thing he's appeared to have fleeced
They're never around, they've all disappeared
I bet he wears glasses and perhaps a false-beard..!

On talking to friends there seems like a pattern
As they report things they've also had happen
They used to play footy for hours each week
Now not a chance as their knees they do creak

Other friends too have mentioned a loss
One that can get them quite terribly cross
On up the stairs on an errand they trek
Then when they get there….'Oh Flippin' Heck..!'

Journey Subject To Change

Their memory of what they'd gone to retrieve
This sneaky old robber, this thought has then thieved
So please look around you, take it all in
As you're never quite sure where he has been

All of your faculties make sure you've got
Check that you can keep an eye on the plot
Before you quite know it, before you catch on
You just might find out that some things have gone

Keep your eyes peeled, watch every day
You're never quite sure what's been took away
But if you think that you're a victim of crime
It could be that sly one, sneaky old 'time'

Lost The Plotto Lotto

Yesterday I played the lotto.
Well it was a special day.
I thought perhaps, you know,
It might bring some luck my way.

Then just this very morning,
Sat an email on my screen.
It proclaimed that I had won,
And my word, how I did dream.

I knew I must stay calm,
I must keep my stuff together.
A yacht, a plane, a Bentley,
I can smell expensive leather..!

Just breathe so slowly in and out,
Keep your feet on solid ground.
I thought of posh apartments,
In New York, how are they found?

Charities would praise my name,
I might start my own foundation,
Those who were less fortunate,
Me! Would thank for its creation.

Well I thought I'd best login,
To see my many millions.
I guess I could employ,
Some people as my minions.

Imagine then just my surprise,
When I saw the princely sum.
About enough to by some 'biccies',
Well, you can stick that up your bum..!

But I'm Perfect

I saw a guy on telly just the other day
He came across all arrogant, all clever and all smart
His face was smug, his hair annoying
I just thought he was a fart…….

Me….of course, I'm perfect, in nearly every way
I can't believe the things I do, most nearly every day

Then there was this woman, she really took the biscuit
She was on a TV quiz and she thought that she should risk it
She lost of course, she lost the lot, silly daft old mare
But there I was just watching as I was sitting there….

Me….of course, I'm perfect, in nearly every way
I can't believe the things I do, most nearly every day

I went to a production of a local show
My friend had asked for charity, so I thought that I should go
The women who were singing, they got the notes all wrong
The fellas in the band could hardly play a gong….!!

Me….of course, I'm perfect, in nearly every way
I can't believe the things I do, most nearly every day

I watched my favourite team playing in the cup
They call themselves professionals, but they all seem to slip-up
All they have to do is to kick a ball and run
If you ask me, what they need, is a kick right up the bum…!!

Me….of course, I'm perfect, in nearly every way
I can't believe the things I do, most nearly every day

Journey Subject To Change

As for art and poetry, don't even get me started
Milton, Keats and Shakespeare, I may as well have farted
The words they use are really bad, have you ever read that stuff?
Picasso, Klimt and Monet their paintings are just 'guff'

Me….of course, I'm perfect, in nearly every way
I can't believe the things I do, most nearly every day

No I've never been on telly and I've not been in a quiz
I've never played in theatre and footballs just a 'swizz'
As for art and poetry, well, that stuff is not for me….
I tell you what I can do…..would you like a cup of tea?

Arriving At.6
Frustrations

We will all experience frustrations on our journeys.

The majority of the things that cause us some frustration will be things that we can have no control over. These things can appear during your journey at any point and from a variety of sources. I sadly have to advise that the bulk of these things are here merely to act as 'splinters under our skin' which we just can't remove.

***Note to Reader – You can at any point double back to 'Daft' if required, before continuing on your way.

Sometimes the best thing we can do is acknowledge them and move on. There are some of these things that we simply cannot bring any change to, at least at that point when we very first encounter them.

There will be others however where we can affect a change and if at all possible we should do.

Change can be as simple as making sure we're extra kind and helpful to someone. At other times it will be raising awareness of things that aren't right, by asking questions and highlighting alternatives, to those who are *allegedly* in charge.

Don't be afraid of asking difficult questions, or for that matter, don't be afraid of asking any questions whatsoever. Sometimes the only way to gain knowledge and understanding of something is to question it.

There's no such thing as a 'stupid question' but there are 'stupid people' who don't ask questions.

You cannot know what you don't know.

Be aware however, there will be some people who do not want to be asked any serious questions at all.

Depending on the situation in play, be prepared for a less than willing recipient and any potential backlash that they could enact. BUT – If you feel the question must be asked, then make sure you wear your 'brave pants' and have a backup plan in place.

Looking after for yourself and your loved ones is the primary goal here.

Can You Tell Me…..?

Why are people horrid?
Why are people cruel?
Why do people fight?
Do I have to go to school?

Can you tell me why
I see the things I do?
Can you tell me what
Am I supposed to do?

I try and do my best
Well…..nearly every day
I try to be quite kind
In nearly every way

I just don't understand
Have I misunderstood?
I just don't understand
Why I have to be so good

It all seems so confusing
It all seems so unfair
I try and do my best
But others just don't care

I guess it might make sense
But at times it's hard to see
I have just one more question
Can you tell me what's for tea?

Journey Subject To Change

I'm Sick

I'm sick of wars and hate
I'm sick of death and fights
I'm sick of seeing on the news
Every single night

People say don't watch the news
Don't look, it makes it better
But that's just being ignorant
As it carries on unfettered

I'll tell you where to start
By calling out the ones you know
Who regurgitate the words of hate
Spreading bile just like snow

I don't care if it's your boss
I don't care if it's a friend
By pointing out their error
Is the way to start the end

The end of all this hatred
The end of all this spite
We're all just human beings
In the cold harsh day of light

Some may be a different colour
Some may be a different sex
Just because they're different
Doesn't make it more complex

Just because they choose
A different way to you
Doesn't mean they're wrong
Doesn't mean your way is true

Journey Subject To Change

I may not like a team in red
I may not like a team in blue
It makes no bloody difference
I'm a human just like you

Sometimes I get it right
Sometimes I get it wrong
I may sing a different harmony
I may sing a different song

Not every little thing in life
Should be labelled wrong or right
Because something is different
Don't mean you have to fight

It really is acceptable
For more than one view to exist
By being narrow minded
New ways we will resist

Bias is the thing
That is getting in the way
We won't listen to that person
We won't hear what they say

Yes it may be different
It may not be what you know
But it could be just as valid
If you give them chance to show

I'm sick of all the cruelty
The hate and prejudice
It's difficult to see
That there is no end to this

Journey Subject To Change

The difference starts today
The difference starts with you
By calling out the things not right
This is something you can do

Be all calm and gentle
Do it in a measured way
Point out to them politely
That there's wrong in what they say

Then move on to other things
You don't need to start a stink
But by questioning their talk
We might just make them think

We need to change beliefs
Or at least say that we're trying
Then things might start to change
Without any others dying

Journey Subject To Change

Male, Pale, Stale

To hear the people speak
I'm apparently to blame
I find it very tough
To carry all this shame
I wish they would remember
That we're not all born the same

By saying what they say
They're just reproducing hate
And kind people of today
They find it hard to take
History is, just what it is
It's the future we must make

Gender, age and colour
Are not an automatic ban
On being someone that
May help with future plans
Nor sex, or sexuality
Don't mean you can't or can

So come on everyone
I thought we were enlightened
And of differences we shouldn't
Be the tiniest bit frightened
Variety and different views
Will make the future brighten

We've got to where we are
And we're better than we were
But to carry on improving
Changes still they must occur
And forgiving one another
Cuts both ways you must concur

Journey Subject To Change

For the world to keep improving
Views of all, they must be heard
To continue on this journey
We must not be deterred
We all have to be open
And the melting pot be stirred

So male, pale, stale is
Behaviour stereotypical
Which all of those who think it
Makes you just as hypocritical
Let's all up our game
Even though it may be difficult

No age, or race or gender
Or any other differential
Mean that someone we don't know
Just doesn't have potential
To close our minds to others
Could miss something essential

Everyone has thoughts to offer
Everyone can play their part
To bring us all a better future
This is surely how we start
So make yourself be open
And do it from the heart

The path we choose the first time
May not always be right
A change in our direction
May give us better sight
But to change for changings sake
Is to be obtuse and trite

Journey Subject To Change

It's easy to be harsh
And it's easy to be cruel
But look a little closer
This makes you the fool
As every single day in life
We're always still in school

Age can bring experience
Youth can give new views
By combing bits of both
The very best we choose
The same can then be said
By having folks in different shoes

So be the change you want to see
The standards you can set
By only looking one way
We're narrowing our bet
And that's how history was
Lest we all forget…..!

By all means have opinions
But realise we must
That sometimes there are others
Whose ideas we must trust
And if it doesn't work
Other ways they must be 'sussed'

We're all in this together
We all must lend a hand
To get a tune worth singing
We must all be in the band
And if it all works out
Then the ending will be grand

Journey Subject To Change

Support your fellow team-mate
No matter who they are
By pulling altogether
It gets us to go far
And in the end when winning
I'll see you at the bar…!

And if somehow we lose
Then our fate do not bemoan
As we all must stay together
For the next seed to be sown
And that is how a future
Which is better can be grown

Platitudes of Pain

I cry sometimes on seeing the pain a human being causes
But prejudice and hate remain no matter what is said
A fight for justice rages on, a fight for changes too
But for all the protestations, and injustices we see, the curse remains

We see bleeding hearts of politicians, as some votes they look to win
Enquiries are launched and root causes are searched out
Yet still we see it, time and again, it never will be gone
Because something is different, because someone doesn't understand

Ignorance it festers and develops into hate

But……..

We're all meant to be different
And the fact that we're all different…..
Means we're also all the same
The consistency of difference links us altogether

We cannot seem to grasp…….
We're all unique in our own way

For a species so enlightened and apparently informed
We cannot let our fellow beings, just be who they are
But bias still exists and hate crimes seem to grow

Will we just continue to not deal with this curse
Will we just continue to see bodies in a hearse

An Empty Well

What can I bring to the world
That is truly of some worth
What can I say? What can I do?
To what on Earth can I give birth?

Therein it lies the question
The one that beats me down
So what is left for me to do?
The question makes me frown

Why do I keep on trying?
When living seems so fearful
Why do I keep lying?
When this life it makes me tearful

I'll wait until the tears have stopped
'Till I see straight again
When the final one has dropped
They've washed away the pain

This isn't as expected
They've rinsed the slates all clean
Perhaps the tears had purpose
As I now see what they mean

Through the cracks within my soul
The droplets have all seeped
It appears that my calling
Has once again been beeped

You cannot solve your puzzle
If you cannot see the clues
Sometimes the path unknown
Is the one that you must choose

Journey Subject To Change

At the end of this new path
Could be a heaven or a hell
But to get the plants of hope to grow
You need water in your well

So now I have a new path
New things I can explore
I'll continue moving forward
Who knows what's through that door?

Journey Subject To Change

Too Cold To Walk

Mum drives round the corner
With her child sat in the seat
In Mum's hand she has her phone
She's looking at a tweet

Got to take my darling one
To the school today
The temperature is chilly
She might freeze upon the way

But she never saw the child
That stepped into the road
Looking at that stupid tweet
Has left one child cold….

Journey Subject To Change

Have you ever wondered

Have you ever wondered
Where you fit within this life?

Have you ever wondered
If all there is, is strife?

Have you ever wondered
Is what I'm doing right?

Have you ever wondered
Why do people fight?

Have you ever wondered
What on earth is all this for?

Have you ever wondered
Am I really meant for more?

Have you ever wondered
Do I need to change?

Have you ever wondered
Why do I feel strange?

Have you ever wondered
Why do I think so much?

Have you ever wondered
Onto dreams why do I clutch?

Have you ever wondered
What if I let this go?

Have you ever wondered
Would anybody know?

Journey Subject To Change

Have you ever wondered……
'Cos I have everyday

Freewill – The Death of Humankind

The storm it had been brewing since the very dawn of time
Humankind had crossed a line, for crime, after crime, after crime

All the deities assembled, the very highest of the high
Unknown to those on Earth, this day would make them cry

Irrespective of the names like Allah, God and more
Today it was the day to settle on the score

The conversation started "I told you this was trouble…"
"I quite agree, that you did, I can see it in the rubble…"

A vote it had been taken, right at the very start
To humankind the deities, a great gift would impart

Freewill it had been granted, from the moment of inception
Humankind, one by one, each choosing their direction

They also had the right to choose to change when 'ere they wish
Little could the future tell, what lay upon that dish…..

"I just don't understand it….." said another gathered there
"How they on Earth, cannot see, all the sadness and despair…?"

"I fear it is more complicated….." another added in….
"They really have not got the strength to live outside of sin…"

Another interjected…"But you hear they know the choices…"
"The problem.." they continued…."is there's just too many voices"

"They know what must be done, but the sin gets in the way"
"From the path of righteousness, they continually will stray"

"The greed, the lust, the gluttony, the wrath and all the rest"
"We just cannot ignore, they will never pass the test…"

The first voice re-commenced "So we're voting once again?"
The rest did all incant "Yes, we're all of the same vein."

The vote was but a blink, the decision it was cast
Humankind had had its time, but now that time had passed

To start again, the only way for wars and hate to end
Humankind had made the choice into chaos to descend

'Project Earth and Humans' – Was the file to put away
What next was the decision, but for another day……

Brave Conversations

If living life was easy then it wouldn't be that precious
The challenges we go through, all bring different stresses
You cannot always see, an ending to the battle
And there will be times, when you feel just like you're cattle

Everyday you're up and at it, an alarm and off to work
The same old thing from day to day, it drives you quite berserk
No matter who you are and no matter what occurs
There's times in life when everything just seems to kind of blur

I know for you, you think, somehow it's kind of worse
But believe me when I say, we all have our own curse
Yes we're super busy and the emails never end
There's so much work to do, it sends you round the bend

But you only get the one life, or that's what I believe
So yes you can work hard, but there's times you need reprieve
Make your feelings known, open up your mouth
It doesn't really matter if it ends up going South

Speak your truth be honest, but do it with respect
Make sure you've thought it through, and took time to reflect
If you think you're really right, you must be true to you
Then go ahead and do it, don't take too long to stew

It might feel rather scary, as to open up is hard
But they'll never understand if you never show your card
You have to be prepared that it might not go as planned
But if you think you're right, then you have to take a stand

I speak from vast experience, sometimes it wasn't nice
But let me tell you this, it is well worth the price
I've maintained some vague respect, of who I really am
I now can clearly see, that they didn't give a damn

Journey Subject To Change

You have to talk it through with the ones who really matter
Make sure you write it down, as your thoughts are prone to scatter
Focus on the message you want to get across
Remember for yourself, you really are your boss

Take a deep breath in, speak slowly, don't be rushed
If you've got things to say, don't let yourself be hushed
Remember to keep breathing, stay calm and keep your cool
You really will not stand to be taken for a fool

So there it is, your prep, you know just what to do
Do it for your loved ones, but especially for you

Arriving At.7
Random

Random stuff, just like 'daft' stuff is essential.

Random is good here and there. You need variety on your journey and this provides a little taster of that. It is always good to have a little 'shuffle' of things. It helps the brain get a little more active. Instead of being in a specific mindset and focused on one main area or topic, it can't quite tell what is coming next and that can be stimulating.

Some of the best things that turn up in your life could be totally random, out of nowhere.

Just like the old saying……..Variety is The Spice of Life

The A B C

Action Brings Change
Don't Ever Forget,
Give Help Incessantly,
Just Keep Learning,
Move, Nourish, Observe,
Perfection's Quite Ridiculous,
Sometimes Time's Unfair,
Variation Worries Xenophobes,
Yesterday's Zero.

The A B C V2

Accept nothing.
Believe no-one.
Check everything.
Do eat healthily.
Exercise regularly.
Forgive freely.
Grab your opportunities.
Hope will help.
Imagination is a must.
Journey far and wide.
Keep your head held high.
Love with all your heart.
Meet hardship with a smile.
Never give up.
Optimism is always useful.
Positivity is essential.
Question yourself regularly.
Respect other people's choices.
Spend only what you can afford.
Trust your own judgement.
Understand others views.
Vehemently defend your rights.
Welcome other opinions.
Xenophobia hurts everyone.
You can never know everything.
Zone out occasionally.

Journey Subject To Change

LLD – Love, Life, Death
So It Begins (Part 1 of 5 Part Piece)

And therein lies the beauty
But that you can't yet see
It doesn't yet encumber you
And that is to be free

The direction now is forward
To where it matters not
Is it this or is it that?
Who cares, my touch is hot

Your focus short, your aim is true
The time it does not matter
What is here is all there is
Just what's upon my platter

So feast and move and move and feast
Nothing ever feels like duty
It doesn't yet encumber you
And therein lies the beauty

LLD – Love, Life, Death
The Energy of Innocence (Part 2 of 5 Part Piece)

All start out in innocence
With no fleeting thought of dark
All boundless, bouncy, full of zest
Their electric charge the spark

But there it is, that unknown thing
Lurking further up the track
You'd have thought that they'd consider it
But they have no time for slack

It sits there dark and broody
Just waiting calm and quiet
Who and when you'll never know
You just cannot deny it

The day arrives, the time is now
And things they have a consequence
All boundless, bouncy, full of zest
All start out in innocence

Journey Subject To Change

LLD – Love, Life, Death
Growth and Yearning (Part 3 of 5 Part Piece)

Time defined and re-aligned
New things await their place
You still don't know what's there beyond
Until it hits you in the face

So wherein once you were suffice
The world has other plans in play
You hit the floor, you're flattened
I Love You are the words they say

One is two and two is new
You're never turning back
You hum, you whir, you crackle
But one more thing you find you lack

Two combined to make a one
Is this what fate designed?
You still don't know what's there beyond
Time defined and re-aligned

LLD – Love, Life, Death
The Silent Lesson (Part 4 of 5 Part Piece)

A prayer, a wish, a whisper
Something so profound
Beyond our feeble human reach
It doesn't make a sound

We cry, we crack, we crumble
It's not meant to be this way
But it matters not what thoughts we hold
For life, it has the final say

Through pain we learn and learn we must
Although a different path we'd choose
So celebrate, enjoy your win
As one by one you lose

It builds, it grows, it ebbs and flows
The lines are now much crisper
Beyond our feeble human reach
A prayer, a wish, a whisper

LLD – Love, Life, Death
Perfect Imperfection (Part 5 of 5 Part Piece)

And therein lies the beauty
You see but just can't touch
A life well lived with highs and lows
You never asked for much

A priceless precious gem you hold
Beyond your comprehension
The joy is in the journey
There is no destination

Again you have a moment
You shine your apple on your sleeve
Things have changed, they're not the same
So relax and slowly breathe

Perfection here is not the goal
Don't do things out of duty
A life well lived with highs and lows
And therein lies the beauty

It's All A Sham – Fame & Fortune

I don't know the things to do
I don't know what's right for you

You've seen some things, you've heard some stuff
But that don't mean you're super tough

Just wait until your world is rocked
Just wait until you're truly shocked

Famous people they come and go
They're just a human don't you know

They don't know any better than you
In their life the path to choose

Money and fame don't buy them happy
It may be different but it could be crappy

Behind the glitz and fame and glamour
The fears, the dread, the headaches clamour

They have more choices that is true
But they also have their pressures too

Take some pills the pain subsides
But the real problems that only hides

So take some more and smile and preen
After all you're living the dream

But dreams can be a nightmare too
And these are the sort that stick like glue

The problem is these dreams are real
Until you take the steps to heal

117

Journey Subject To Change

To us outside it all looks swell
But if it's your dream, it's a living hell

We only see the sanitized glory
We don't see the real story

That is till it falls apart
And the whole wide world sees their bleeding heart

We talk and gossip and laugh and chatter
While that person's life begins to shatter

We always knew they were no good
Underneath their diamond encrusted hood

We enjoyed the good and we love the pain
It makes us feel that they're just the same

But that's the thing we need to remember
As their lives we start to dismember

They never were any better than us
We're just glad they're under the bus

Feeling Scared – Fear – Uncertainty – The Question

I have to tell you…………….

Inside myself today, I'm feeling rather funny
I've got this sort of tickle deep inside my tummy

It isn't very nice and I don't know what it is
Also in my head, everything just seems to fizz

I have so many things that are whizzing round my brain
There seems so many things that could cause me so much pain

I hear it on the news, I see it every day
It's like these nasty things will just not go away

Things like war and illness, bad people, earth in danger
Fighting and unhappiness and don't talk to a stranger

There are some more as well, that also make me worry
Like why my bestest friend, away from me did hurry?

Exams and all my homework I'm not sure I'll do too well
And then there was this nasty kid who told me 'Go to hell!'

I feel like I'm a loser, I'm stupid and I'm daft
I wish that I could fly away in my very own spacecraft

No-one really likes me, I'll be judged and I'll be bullied
I think that you could say, I'm feeling rather worried

I want to cry, I want to hide, I want to run away
I want to be so clever and know just what to say

But I really just don't know, how to deal with all of this
I know it won't just go away if I make a special wish

Journey Subject To Change

So I really would be grateful if you could find the time
To help me understand these things within my rhyme

Feeling Scared – Fear – Uncertainty – What To Do

Firstly let me say, you really are quite smart
The best thing you can do, is to open up your heart

Telling me the things you have, really is quite brave
From these fears and worries, you, together we will save

All the things you've mentioned I really understand
And to cope with all this stuff a route can now be planned

The thing with television, social media and the news
Is they cram this stuff together so it's always in our views

That makes these things seem worse, like it's really never ending
It really would be better if love and kindness they were sending

But still, bad things do happen and that I won't deny
Some things they are so sad that indeed they make you cry

There are some things however that all of us can do
By being kind and helpful we can help each other through

But please try to remember that the world is large and wide
And whilst these things do happen it's not right by your side

It's very normal to be sad, when bad things you see and hear
The way to make it through, is with friends and family near

You also must remember that people can be kind
Sometimes we have to try and make sure it's those we find

If you think of all the good things you've got so close to you
I'm sure that you will find, these things will help you through

The way to make things better is to share how you are feeling
Don't keep it in, all stuffed inside, let it out like there's no ceiling

Find a special someone, a someone you can trust in
As by sharing all your fears, then with truth the lies you're busting

So here we are, we're at the end, although we're at the start
Find a person you can trust and open up your heart......

Understanding's Overrated

Everyone's the same, everyone's unique
He said unto himself as he thought himself a freak
Was there any comfort to be extracted from this thought?
He struggled for an answer as his inner-demons fought

Is there any good to be gained from introspection?
Or is it yet another thing, from where I feel infection?
The questions they were racking up, another and another
The failure that I think I am, will these questions cover?

There again another one, he answered with a question
Perhaps he thought, I'll try again, this time with a suggestion
Questions haven't solved it, my friend you know this true
This time I'll try another tack, with feelings I'll imbue

With a prism held up to his thoughts, he cast his gaze again
He looked upon himself this time, just like an alien
These things you think, he thought, it can't be overstated
For one's own health my friend, understanding's overrated…..

Not All Beer And Skittles…

I look at all these rockstars and movie stars as well.
I think, 'Oh Wow, they've got a life, it really must be swell'.

Then you hear about the drugs and the alcohol as well.
So then I start to wonder, perhaps it's really hell?

I know I generalize and some have got it 'sussed'.
But when you look at fame, you wonder who they trust.

Nearly everyone you meet, perhaps they're on the take?
Who of them are real ? Who of them are fake?

Then I think again and decide that you know what?
I'll leave it up to them, I'm happy with my lot.

The Last Place You Look

I'd been trying to find myself for so long, I got lost along the way.

The years had ebbed away whilst my search continued and still no luck.

I decided the time had come to stop trying to find myself…..

Imagine my surprise…………

Weirdly, there I was, exactly where I'd left myself previously, all those years ago.

I was there all along, right where I was supposed to be.

Who would have thought!

Funny isn't it?

You always find it in the last place you look.

The Lark Ascending Has Its Time

The violinist stands and gently sways, as the strings she bows with a touch so deft

Eyelids closed do flicker, in time with tune and notes that sing and dance

The lark it is ascending, then swooping down again, my heart responds and soars away and my mind begins to drift

The notes or chords, whatever they're called have carried me away

The sound of strings melodic captivate my heart

If I were not sat upon this chair I too would surely sway

Entranced, bewitched and bothered, by the incantation weaved

I believe again the world has beauty.......but again I've been deceived

The world is harsh and cruel and the dissonance quite mocking

Right now however, I will remain, deep inside this moment, the world will still be there when the music comes to rest

Everything must have its time, of this you can be sure

But now the Lark's Ascending and this joy is oh so pure........

Journey Subject To Change

Daily Affirmation For Two

*(To be performed in a power stance ((hands on hips, standing with legs slightly apart, facing each other)) to enhance the feeling of taking control of the day and rotating hips, alternating direction, to start the body moving.)

Today I'm going to be my best self
You're going to be your best self
We're going to do a day's Monday in a day's Monday**
Shine, bright, happy, positive, strong
Full of Fortitude
Just going with the flow
Sending out love
Receiving love
Lots of self-care
And knowing we're there for each other
Being careful when we go out
Not touching too many things
Staying away from silly people
But knowing
Whatever happens
WE CAN DO IT…..!!

(Bump tummies and kiss and hug)***

* Optional physical movement – Recommended But Can Be Tailored to Individual Preferences
**Inserting the necessary / different days as you do it
***Optional physical conclusion – Recommended But Can Be Tailored to Individual Preferences

Arriving At.8
Deep Thinkers

Being a deep thinker isn't a choice, it's just the way you're built, it is who you are.

It can be both a blessing and a curse.

You love to try and make a difference, to solve problems, you care deeply.

You want to help others, you want to make things better for everyone. You have really high standards which can be difficult to achieve all the time, but you have to try. You hold deep beliefs, albeit sometimes it's difficult to fully articulate what it is you believe in, there's just something there which drives you on.

You have a strong moral compass and feel things very deeply. Life has to have purpose and meaning and you want to do nothing more than be a force for good.

The downside to being such a conscientious and caring soul, is the fact that the world in reality can be very harsh.

This makes many of the things you see difficult to understand and process, as they are so at odds with how you view the world.

This leads to times when you experience a surge in these troubling emotions and they are hard to handle.

These feelings will pass, these moods will move on. Like the dark clouds that they feel like they are, the sun is still there, it's just hidden from view for a short time.

You must believe in yourself, you care so much, because you have so much to give.

Let the storm clouds pass and you will shine again.

The Iceberg of Despair

Today I'm like an iceberg that's broken off a glacier.

If I drifted into warmer waters then perhaps my pain would melt......

Could it be that ten percent is really all you see?
You cannot see the rest below which is slicing into me.
You cannot see the jagged shards with edges just like razors.
You cannot see beneath my surface, how they stab into my soul.

My emotions they are freezing, below the part that you can see.
As underneath is where I am, drifting in a frozen barren sea.
Like an iceberg I deteriorate, through melting and through fracture.
Cast adrift as I've been battered by the sea of my misfortune.

An iceberg can capsize at any moment without warning.
Will I make it through the night, will I make it to the morning?
The glacier that I called home, forced against me, made me split.
My world began to fracture and I drift away from shore.

At times when I am quiet, as my mood it lies down flat.
'Tabular' it is my name if you want to be exact.
Sometimes I am 'brash' and at others I'm a 'growler'.
That is when my anger is my evil lurking prowler.

Just below the surface is where the mortal dangers hide.
My ship it sails too close and the ice punctures my pride.
The tearing of my hull renders useless my defences.
I now no longer have control of the rudder of my senses.

No lifeboats have been stowed away, no buoy can save this boy.
This isn't just a film and I am not a toy.
The flares have been extinguished, no lights will sear the sky.
A bobbing figure you won't see.........this life begins to die.

Journey Subject To Change

Drifting like an iceberg with no power or direction.
No lifeguards can be called to help in my protection.
No mayday and no morse code, no beeps and dots or dashes.
There are no further sounds, my hope sinks in silent splashes…..

The breach below the water line was deep and it was fatal.
He sank without a trace, whilst he stood in front of you.
He drifted in the dark and there's nothing you can do…..

Be watchful for an iceberg, keep your radar keen.
They might just need a shoulder which is warm on which to lean…..

131

The Shifting Sands of Love

"I feel that our relationship has moved to a new level"
Were the words that hung there in the air
But at his face, into his eyes, I just could not stare
I wasn't sure quite what he meant, was this good or bad?

This statement felt impromptu, silence was my choice
I left them there to float in air, to see just where they'd land
To marinate, let the flavour build, was this something grand
I wasn't sure where he was going, a commitment or desertion?

More words they weren't forthcoming, where now did we stand?
I glanced so briefly up and saw the look upon his face
I wasn't sure that we were heading into a better place
More words from me just wouldn't help, as eggshells lay ahead

Into treacle thick as it could be, time now it had entered
The seconds passed like hours, the silence hurt my ears
Was I headed for a future bright, or was it my worst fears?
His lips they parted slightly, I waited for my fate…..

But that's the thing sometimes, you really have to……….wait
I heard the air seep from his mouth in a gentle yet deep sigh
No words were coming, his mouth it closed and a tear rolled from
his eye
Should I touch it, wipe away the feelings seeping out?

Resolute is how I stayed, he needed time to think
I knew he wasn't, he knew I wasn't, going anywhere
This thing that we had started, like a flame it needed air
We moved as one together, the stairs beneath our feet

We rose in steady unison, quite why I wasn't sure
The crisp night air it greeted me as we made it to the roof
The thing with love is that sometimes, you need to see some proof
The city stared right back to meet the gaze we cast

Journey Subject To Change

Our future and to where we'd head I would now know at last
Sitting softly, breathing slow, his head now in his hands
I thought of distant places, of different foreign lands
The sun, the moon, the faces, the places we had been

Together facing everything, always we both were there
That is when I knew it, I felt that icy stare
A turn, a step onto the ledge, a crouch then power from the legs
No looking back, or looking up there was no-one left to see

You see, the two was one, the one was I, alone again with me
The new level of relationship, was a milestone I had reached
No more words, just action, my hopes had all been beached
I flew on wings invisible and landed on my own……..

The flight was swift, the landing hard, there was no coming back
Depression has a knowing way to feed on what you lack
The void where love just might have grown, can fill a heart and mind
So with each and every one you meet, remember to be kind

Positivity

The reason that you worry, is because you really care
No matter what the people think, let them stop and stare

It's you that really matters, you're the star in your own show
The fears and all the worries, you've just got to let them go

If you're doing what you think you should, then that's the thing that counts
If the people just don't like it, then your name let them renounce

Because it doesn't matter what the other people think
Just stare them out, face to face, and wait for them to blink

Let them make their move, let them do just as they will
Be yourself and no-one else, it's really quite a thrill

Being your own person, living your own life
Do it how you want to do, it just removes the strife

Ignore the rubbish out there, ignore the haters too
Be consistent in your actions and do what you must do

Be authentic and be kind and to others do no harm
Put only goodness out there and it comes back like a charm

Be open and be honest and take heed of other folk
Some they will be quality and some just a like a joke

Take notice of the good stuff, build your knowledge with good care
And slowly you will realise that it's no good to compare

We all have skills and talents and no two exact the same
And if some things don't quite work out, then don't apportion blame

Journey Subject To Change

Everyone can learn something, if things they don't work out
But pointing fingers doesn't help, don't scream and please don't shout

Develop for the next time, add experience to your bank
And when you are victorious it's the wisdom you can thank

Wisdom is expensive though, there is a cost to pay
Learning from experience as you move from day to day

There really are no shortcuts to earn this valued thing
You have to learn the lyrics if you really want to sing

Flying in a plane and far out into space
Once they were unheard of, but now they're commonplace

Experiments were done, before success was found
Many will have failed and come crashing to the ground

If you believe it's worth the risk to do the thing you dare
Then trying is the only way to truly get you there

Those who never fail in life, have never really tried
A bump, a bruise that's all they are, it really is just pride

Be positive, be brave, your life is not yet written
Adventuring's the only way, explore just like a kitten

Being nervous is quite normal, there's nothing wrong with that
Be kitten-like as you explore and you'll grow into a cat

A scar or two you may pick up, but that's to be expected
That's life's way of showing all the wisdom you've collected

Positivity's the major thing you need as you explore
As you never really know what is coming through your door

Journey Subject To Change

With your shield of positivity, you can face a daunting task
With the knowledge there's a chance, that in success you'll bask

You take it not for granted, for that would just be daft
But if this thing should sink, then you know you've got a raft

So there you go, that's all there is, I have no special prize
The rest my friend is up to you as you'll slowly realize

The way into the future is to journey for yourself
Take care in what you choose and be careful with your health

As you move along your chosen path through this crazy thing called life
You'll encounter good and bad, yes I'm sorry that stuff's rife

It cannot be avoided though, it's through that stuff we learn
Take care with all you meet and your bridges do not burn

I know that this is difficult, 'cos life's a mystery
So always have it with you, your positivity

The Accuser Accused

I looked my accuser straight in the eye
I tried my damndest to really not cry
How could they say just what they'd said?
People like that deserve to be dead

I turned my face and closed my eyes
I thought that a winner was one who tries?
That they had said though, was not the truth
And to fail yet again, was yet further proof

I know that they spoke of things that were so
But just at this moment I wished they would go
No not a chance, they wouldn't relent
To destroy my esteem they were truly intent

They did have a point, there's no point in being
If you produce things that no-one is seeing
Save us all time, spare us a thought
There's so many things you needn't have bought

They started again, they just stated facts
A person is judged by the way that they act
I knew they were right, I'd wasted their time
And to do such a thing was the greatest of crimes

I took a deep breath and turned back around
There they were stood, where I knew they'd be found
Yet once again they stared in my eye
They wondered perhaps if this time I'd cry?

No, not this time, I know there's no point
My guilt, they and I, our agreement was joint
Stating 'OK, it's time to move on'
My hopes of a future were totally gone

Journey Subject To Change

I'd entered with hope, I'd entered with verve
But when you've no talent, that takes quite a nerve
I sprayed out the polish and raised up the duster
This mirror I thought had lost all its lustre....

Journey Subject To Change

The Cloud

The cloud arrived again today and stopped above my head
Sorry, no I mean to say, I was cloaked in robes of dread
It wrapped itself around me with a vice-like iron grip
Into my veins its poison went, in a constant steady drip

I want to fight, I want to win, but yet I cannot muster
My resistance it just don't exist, it's like a feather duster
It's feeble, weak, and hardly there and is gone in just a blink
Perhaps the tonic that I need is just another drink

No, I know that's not the answer, that will not help me out
I want to fight I really do, I want to scream and shout
But as the dust of disappointment settles lightly on my skin
It forms into a crust so hard, there's no chance I can win

So settle down and let it be, it has to have its time
It's the jailor, this is jail and having fun it was my crime
I had my fun and more than most, so the price it must be paid
But unlike dragons in the films this beast it can't be slayed

And therein lies the secret and a chink of light I see
Be patient, wait it out and I know that I'll return to me
I lie down to be ravaged and my dreams all torn to shreds
But garments, robes and finery, they all start out as threads

Dragon's flames they burn so fierce, scorch my soul to ash
My thoughts and plans, good intentions thrown out in the trash
It hurts, it burns, it spares no pain, as shards they pierce my thoughts
Like the battle for some justice that is fought out in the courts

So wriggle not, just hideaway and keep your head quite low
Quicksand grabs the more you fight so take it nice and slow
The less you feed this hungry demon, the less energy it has
Hide your instruments away today, so it cannot play its jazz

Journey Subject To Change

You feel a tiny movement, the smallest twitch somewhere inside
It's like you've seen the rarest bird from your personal bird hide
It moved, I saw it but now it's gone, but I know its roundabouts
Just keep it quiet and steady and make sure that no-one shouts

The threads are there, you know they are, you need a handful more
The music notes are also there, but enough to make a score?
Then out of nowhere like a breeze, your hope raises its head
Perhaps the day is not all lost, you may not wind up dead

The breeze it has a promise that you hope that it can keep
Like the dogs within a field as they gather up the sheep
It blows a little stronger and the rays of sun shine through
The cloud it starts to move away and there you are, there's you.

Journey Subject To Change

Peace and Introspection

A time of introspection
is what's needed now you know
A place of peace and quiet
where my mind and I can go

Somewhere where we're welcome
to just be who we are
Somewhere nice and close
I don't want to use the car

A time of introspection
A time for peace and calm
A time and place for me alone
Where I do myself no harm

A time to sow the seed
of belief in what I've done
A time to praise myself
for just how far I've come

Let the chaos settle
let the chatter stop
Time to just be thankful
for everything I've got

The Revelation of Despair

No-one really has a clue what the hell life's all about.

A sneer arrived upon my face as I contemplated where I fitted into the world, because…

The futility of me actually trying to do something of worth, landed with a weight I could no longer bear.

My vaingloriousness had circled back around and slapped me in the face with the force of a tsunami yet unrivalled or experienced.

Once again it lay waste to any feelings of worth, spread as thin as goldleaf, but with none of the appeal or lustre of its simile.

The hours, days, weeks and months of work merely served to exacerbate my feelings of worthlessness.

The dark, dank cave of my self-loathing was I discovered, firmly available for my use via my own internal version of a popular BNB booking site.

The irony of its acronym amused me with its accuracy,

Anything **I**s **R**arely **B**eyond **N**arcissistic **B**uggery.

I had quite literally, shafted myself with my own belief.

Still, the sneer remained, emboldened by the headache that now carved my skull in two.

I'd have wiped my feet on the filth-laden doormat that awaited my arrival, but, as this was the entrance to where I would once again be staying for an indeterminate amount of time, I didn't want to miss the opportunity to add to the fetid and pungent ambience that would once again greet me.

'Despair' – What an interesting name adorned the frame as I entered. I had the sneaking feeling that this was where I'd started to discover what life was all about the last time I was here……

"Oh Goody…" I thought, "Life is just about to enlighten me, loathing here I come…..!!"

The Futility of Existence

What happens when you realise…
That irrespective of whether or not,
You're doing something specific,
Life is totally futile!

It makes zero difference,
Everything makes zero difference,
No matter how important you feel your work is,
It is totally futile!

It makes less than a blink,
Of a difference to anything…..
We do all this work…..
For whatever reason

We do all this worrying…..
About what it doesn't matter
We strive to be something…..
Whatever that may be, and…..

It makes not a blind bit of difference.

Surely upon this realization you know….

I can do whatever I want
I can be whatever I choose to be
Whatever I do or achieve
How insignificant that may appear to anyone else

Is truly a thing to be celebrated

I am me
I did this

This is mine……..forever

I've Done Some Things

I've done some things of which I'm not proud
I've shouted at people and screamed right out loud
I've sought justification for what I have done
And I see provocation where there ought to be none

I didn't want to cause pain, I want no-one to suffer
But that includes me, I was fooled by a bluffer
Innocent maybe, I want us all to do well
Then I discovered some instigate hell

Many years later with the pain still inside
They incanted a curse from which I can't hide
I can't understand why in torment I live
And why it is me, who's supposed to forgive

I offered forgiveness and it came from my heart
It was me who got poisoned right at the start
The badness came out as the fever had peaked
But it's others from whom forgiveness is seeked

Foolish and futile the pursuit of a pardon
As a bully their heart has already hardened
And this is the point where I start to see through
The lies and the hatred they started to brew

No matter the torture I had to endure
I continue to try and keep my heart pure
Whilst I'm never all right, I'm never all wrong
So I lift up my head, fill the world full of song

The day when I start to stop even trying
Is the start of the end, it's when I start dying
So I offer forgiveness to myself deep within
I'll continue to face the world with a grin

Journey Subject To Change

I'll try and be kind and to help where I can
I'll even keep trying if things head off plan
So whilst I'm not proud of some things I've done
I know that the darkness still hasn't won

I know that utopia doesn't really exist
But I'll try to do good, I just can't resist
All I can hope for from my fellow folk
Is to keep spreading love and living in hope

Deep Down Inside

Where do I go when the world goes all quiet
To the back of my brain where rages a riot
I am the one who smiles and laughs
Who creates such a giggle with deliberate gaffs

I am the uncle, the brother, the friend
For whom the chaos just never ends
You can't see it there, right there in my face
It's hidden within a dark secret place

To spare the world the pain deep within
Is why you see me wearing a grin
You've enough going on in your own life
Without me sharing with you all my strife

A burden is not what I want to be
That's why I will limit just what you see
So carry on by, there's nothing to see
Just crazy old him, being crazy old he

He's daft and he's whacky, he's always been that
But deep down inside he's incredibly flat
He's oh so deflated, there seems no more point
In carrying on ....

Journey Subject To Change

Anger

Anger is a curious thing, I'll explain just why that's so…..

Some days I don't see it
Those are days I crave
Then days when it is here
It engulfs me like a wave

The days when I don't see it
I wonder where it goes?
The days when it engulfs me
Well, it's all I really know

When my anger sits there with me
I want to rant, I want to rage
I want everything destroyed
I should be locked up in a cage

I growl at chirping birds
I wish the sun would go away
I want to smash, destroy and burn
All the things within my way

But that there is the problem
The thing that makes me mad
If I let out all my rage
Then it's 'me' who suffers bad

If I vented all my anger
And exploded like a bomb
It wouldn't make things better
It's 'my pain' it would prolong

Journey Subject To Change

You see, now that is funny
That's the thing that makes it worse
If I let out all my anger
It's like I've doubled my own curse

I would be the one
That would receive the blame
I would be the one
Who got burned by my own flame

By trying to release
All my anger physically
The person that I hurt the most
Primarily is me

People wouldn't like me
I'd get told off here and there
I would be the one
At whom the people stare

Then I'd feel quite horrid
For being so annoying
I would also feel bad
For all the things I'd been destroying

So on the days when I feel anger
I try to be quite calm
I'm careful what I do
I try not to cause alarm

I try and be quite peaceful
I try to take things........slow
I'm careful what I say
I don't want to let it blow

Journey Subject To Change

And 'yes' some things annoy me
I may feel my anger grow
But that can be quite positive
As to beat it, then I know…..

I need to take a moment
I need to take a breath
If I let it all fly out
I'll only cause a mess

Then I'll try and laugh at it
I know that may sound strange
But when I say 'You're here again'
'Aren't there flowers to arrange?'

It's like, it makes it seem less fierce
Like it isn't all that bad
If daft things I keep saying
I might return to 'glad'

So yes it is quite normal
To feel anger and feel cross
But if you think of fluffy things
Then the anger's not the boss

Some days are a challenge
Some days they're a breeze
Some days are quite hot
And on other days you freeze

And that's the same with anger
It's here and then it's not
And if you can just ride it out
Then quickly it's forgot

Journey Subject To Change

Just know that this is normal
But remember you can win
Breathe and think of funny things
And you might just see a grin

If a grin you see
Then grab and hold on tight
Because by laughing and a-joking
Then things will be alright

It's the same with stress and sadness
And other things not nice
They will occur from time to time
But double-not the price

By thinking and a-worrying
They may be on their way
Instead of liking here and now
Another price you pay

So…..today it is a good day
I'm here I've got a chance
I can make it all the better
If I face it with a dance

The dance can be inside yourself
You don't have to actually do it
But dancing, smiles and laughter
They will always see you through it

So there it is my anger
This weird and curious thing
When it arrives, I will depart
To go and have a sing……

Deep Breath, Count To Ten

Today I give up, today I am lost
My mind for some reason a line it has crossed

I started to think, I really did try
But right there and then my mind said 'Goodbye'

Off it did wander down some winding lane
And none of the good thoughts came back the same

It's one of those days where you hold your hands up
It's clear to see that I've emptied my cup

We all have a day where you have to accept
Out of the back door your thoughts have all crept

So I'll cut me some slack, I'll call it a day
From the bank of my mind I've nothing to pay

I'll see you tomorrow, we'll try once again
But for now a deep breath and counting to ten

Fight Night

As the silence settles in, for what it thinks will be the night
That is when the voices gather and decide that they will fight
They gather in a corner and stay silent in their hiding
They await the most destructive time to finally start fighting
They jockey for position, with their silent slippers on
They know that if they peak too soon, disruption will be gone
My breathing slows and deepens, the time it is approaching
They know within themselves my sleep they'll be encroaching
Time though is their friend, they've got time to kill
They'll wait until the time is right, and for me to be quite still
An hour or two slide slowly by, they fidget and they jostle
They wait just like religion, searching for their next apostle
Then revelation, lo behold, the chosen one is here
It bellows loud and deep, hard within my inner ear
It trumpets like an army man, blowing hard upon his bugle
Like a rich man splashing cash 'Oh yes' he isn't frugal
He delivers all that he can give, he's started quite a melee
Soon I will discover, he's woken growls within my belly
The voices that have gathered, seize upon the mass confusion
And deep inside my head, they wish to cause a large contusion
That is it, the fight commences, hell breaks loose within my head
I start to toss and turn, no more peace within my bed
Random words and phrases, thoughts I thought had all but gone
Sold me on a promise, of sound sleep, but that's a con
Dancing like a dancer wearing clogs of solid steel
As their fight it rages on they don't care just how I feel
Bouncing off the inside of my crazy cranium
It seems as if these thoughts are really having fun
Numbers too appear, as equations to be solved
My sleep like headache tablets has now but all dissolved
I raise my tired frame, and out of bed to make some tea
My thoughts they seem to settle in their corner full of glee
Their work just for the moment, has been executed well
They bide their time before once again, delivering their hell

Journey Subject To Change

And so this is my pantomime, or my play all full of farce
They gather up their instruments to make my sleep quite sparse
As rituals go, this isn't quite what I had really planned
But as I say, they sold me sleep, but I know that I've been scammed
I just hope that there's a bruiser of a thought within the scheme
Perhaps it may just knock these thoughts into some sort of dream
I hug my pillow, snuggle in, and hope that there's a chance
That for tonight the dancers, have danced their final dance…

Comeback Song

I don't want to do today
I'm finding it quite hard
It's like my motivation
Has been given a red card

I'm getting thoughts I do not want
I've got emotions running wild
I'm going to lose my shit
I'm behaving like a child

It's irrational and stupid
I know 'coz I'm grown up
And there isn't any reason
I wish these thoughts would stop

They don't, they keep on coming
I don't need them in my head
I'm trying to be rational
But I wish that I was dead

I don't, I'm being stupid
I can't help myself today
But I really really wish
That these thoughts would go away

I'm angry and I'm cross
I'm resentful and I'm hurt
I wish there was a happy spray
I possessed that I could squirt

There are days when I see magic
I see goodness everywhere
But today is just a day
When I couldn't really care

Journey Subject To Change

I don't need someone to tell me
Just get out, do this or that
Just stay away from me
Or I'm going to knock you flat

I just have to work on through it
I have to keep my head down low
I just need to let them be
And tomorrow they will go

There are times when I can shake it
There are times when I cannot
There are times I'm altogether
And there's others when I'm not

I know this is my way
I know that this is me
I really cannot force it
I have to let it be

So please just give me space
Please just give me room
Today there are no flowers
And I cannot see them bloom

I know this isn't helpful
I know this isn't right
But today is just a day
When I haven't any fight

There's really nothing more
That's all there is to say
No need to make a drama
So just be on your way

Journey Subject To Change

I'm fine I will get over it
I know it's quite irrational
And no, I am not doing it
To try and be quite fashionable

I wish I could get over it
I wish it would go quicker
But trust me I'm a flame
I get low but I still flicker

Check in on me again
By all means please return
And then you'll see again
Just how brightly I can burn

So, before you burn your fingers
It's time for you to go
And if I really need you
Be sure I'll let you know

I'll be back with a vengeance
My return it will be loud
All belief and positivity
Oh trust me, you'll be proud

So there you see already
It's just beneath the surface
We all have days like this
When we feel like we are worthless

So please, enough already
We must be moving on
I'll catch up with you tomorrow
When you hear my comeback song

Arriving At.9
Wisdom

There is a flip side to the difficult emotions you may experience.

More than most, you tend to come through things in such a way, that you can see the wisdom that you have gained from travelling through those tough times.

You have this gift for being able to place value on the things that really do matter in life.

You can see through superficiality with ease.

One of the most valuable nuggets of wisdom that you have to remember, is the fact that for you, above all others, you have to cut yourself some slack.
You're really doing rather well.

Take a step back and have a look. I think you'll see that you've already made a good deal of positive progress and you should be rightly proud of this.

Afraid of Now

Please don't be afraid of now, it's all you've truly got
I know it can be scary and sometimes you lose the plot

But please just take a breath, and to yourself be true
Look how far you've come and all that you've been through

Previously you've had hard times and yet now here you are
By being strong and brave before, its brought you oh so far

So gather up your courage, it's there somewhere inside
It's just playing hard to get, in a corner it does hide

You'll find it as you've done before and bring it into play
And by using all your skill and strength you'll make it through today

OK I know it can be hard, and some days take the mickey
And this one's took the biscuit too, it's feeling rather tricky

But breathe again and close your eyes and tell yourself it's so
You simply won't be beaten, up and onwards you will go

Open eyes and breathe again let your shoulders feel relaxed
You'll be riding through these waves like a surfboard that's been waxed

A tad too much, yes maybe, but you're getting the impression
That to yourself you're giving, a little 'pep' talk session

It works as well you know, you're feeling that bit braver
If you truly trust yourself, you are your own life saver

Tongue-tied yes, but that's the trick to get the mind to focus
Distract the rubbish thoughts with a little hocus-pocus

Journey Subject To Change

And here you are, once again, you're back into the game
Now you know the way it works you'll never be the same

Keep your home fires burning, make sure they're really hot
But please don't be afraid of now, it's truly all you've got

Change

Change is not a choice
It is a daily must
And truly there's just one
In whom to place your trust

Change is not a choice
It's not optional you know
Change it is essential
To get yourself to grow

Change it is your friend
As it's you who drives the train
As only you control
What you keep within your brain

Change will take you places
You never could have dreamt
So make your changes wisely
Do not treat them with contempt

Change can be a challenge
Oh yes my friend, it's true
But please do not forget
What change can do for you

Change, it can be good
Or change, it can be bad
Consider all your options
And choose what makes you glad

Choosing not to change
Is an option there for you
But changing what you want
Will bring new things to you

Journey Subject To Change

Choice is not a luxury
Please don't believe that lie
We can all choose what we change
If we really want to try

Change it is essential
You change each and every day
So change the way you think
Start that change today

Journey Subject To Change

Perspectives

You can see what I can see, but your view is for you.
I may see the same thing, but from a different view.

You may see a plant, all thriving and all green.
Whereas I may see a weed and a path that needs a clean.

I may see a concert with the music loud and great.
You may wish they'd quieten down, it really is quite late.

You may see a cat, fluffy, cute and always purring.
I may see a pest as the birds it is disturbing.

I may see a child singing jolly songs all playful.
You may hear a child whose singing is distasteful.

That is just a few of the things we could see different,
but it really is no use to be upset and all belligerent.

There is no single person with opinions always right,
but this isn't any reason that anyone should fight.

By being kind and caring and the sharing of our views,
it can help the other people understand the things we choose.

It doesn't mean that we are right and they are wrong.
Sometimes it takes a choir to make a better song.

Understanding can be difficult, agreement's not the aim.
But respecting one-another, is the aim of this here game.

So perspectives can be different, there's nothing wrong with that.
But it doesn't have to start a war, with an unnecessary spat.

Agree to disagree but respect the others view,
and they alike must also respect the view of you.

So I have my perspective, you can have yours too,
and in peaceful disagreement we may all just make it through.

Journey Subject To Change

Good Days

There are things within this world
That I don't understand
There are things that happen in my life
I hadn't really planned

But this you see is normal
This just.......is how life is
It can't be planned or written
It's not a test or quiz

Some days I feel lonely
Some days I just feel lost
Some days I wonder why
And how much this all will cost

Do I have the money
In the bank inside my head
Or will it cost too much
And will I wind up dead?

Other days are triumphs
I feel like I'm the best
These are days of wonder
I greet them with such zest

But then they go like mist
They evaporate so quick
Like someone changed the page
With a damned annoying 'click'

When days are full of wonder
Fast forward's how they go
And when they will return
It's not for us to know

Journey Subject To Change

So if you get a good one
One that's smiles and fun
Get yourself fresh air
Get yourself out in the sun

Be careful how you do it
Don't go out, without your cream
And in the blazing sun
Do not fall asleep and dream

Instead stay wide awake
Drink in this day of wonder
For all too quick you know
It will be put asunder

Be grateful for the good days
You never can be sure
If you will get another
Come knocking at your door

The Tomorrow Scam

I've heard about this thing, it's terrible I know
I'll tell you all about it and just how this does go

They promise you tomorrow, like somehow it's really there
But you'll never really see it, no matter how you stare

They pretend that it exists and it's yours for you to take
But listen to my words, what they're offering is fake

It's illusion, it's unreal, I was sold the dream as well
And now I'm really locked in this never ending hell

I'm always in today, there is just no escape
You'll never be a superman and have a flashy cape

So heed my words and watch your step, listen to my tip
The day to keep your eye on, might just give you the slip

The day that needs a-watchin' and concentrating on
Is the one that's always with you, the one that's never gone

That day is today, as it's all that's real and true
Just try your very best, as that's all that you can do

So while there's no real harm, in a hoping for tomorrow
Believing in today is the way to banish sorrow

So hoping in tomorrow as a thing, yes, that's OK
But never stop believing in the day that is today

Some Days

Some days you need forgiving.
Some days you must forgive.
Some days you want to die.
Some days you want to live.

Some days are the hardest.
Some days are the best.
Some days they are easy.
Some days they're a test.

Some days last forever.
Some days go so quick.
Some days you're the flame.
Some days you're the wick.

Some days stay right with you.
Some days fade without a trace.
Some days kindness finds you.
Some days strain your grace.

Some days love is with you.
Some days love is scarce.
Some days love is gentle.
Some days love is fierce.

Some days see you build.
Some days see you crumble.
Some days see you proud.
Some days see you humble.

Some days seem ignorable.
Some days we don't choose.
Some days winning's easy.
Some days we just lose.

Journey Subject To Change

Some days are a blessing.
Some days are a curse.
Some days could be better.
Some days could be worse.

Some days give you answers.
Some days we're just lost.
Some days we are lucky.
Some days take their cost.

Some days looking back.
Some days surging on.
Some days they are here.
Some days they are gone.

So Many Questions

I've got so many things all flying round my mind
I've got so many questions and the answers I can't find

I drive myself quite 'scatty', my brain cannot relax
Until I find them all, the truth, the answers…facts

But then a question most obscure comes firmly into focus
Should my brain, like a field of corn, be ravaged by these locusts?

And that is when an answer, just one, comes to my aid
To know it all's not possible and I shouldn't be afraid

And there it is the only thing, I truly need to know
To know it all's impossible I need to let it go……

I consider it a little more, to check out every angle
I look above, below and through, as this question I do wrangle

But there it is, as clear as day, it stands up to the test
You never can know everything, you can only do your best

I know that this is said a lot, they say it all the time
In fact I can't believe it, I say it in this rhyme…….

But take it from an expert in mind-mismanagement
There are a load of questions from your brain that you should shunt

By all means keep a few that you really want to ponder
But brains they just work better, if they've got some room to wonder….

Patience

Be patient with yourself above all others

Be patient with your ideas

Be patient, let them form and the basis solidify

Be patient, given time, the words will come

Be patient, time doesn't rush on by, we only think it does

Be patient, what's meant for you won't pass you by

Be patient, if the door doesn't open, perhaps it's not your door

Be patient, the disappointment of today can be the nugget of success for tomorrow

Be patient, it may just be a nugget but given time and love it could grow

Be patient, an embryo of an idea can develop beyond your wildest imagination

Be patient, the ending will arrive when the time is right

Be patient, an ending can be the beginning of something else magnificent

Be patient, forcing it, when it isn't ready doesn't work, it just builds frustration

Be patient, the frustration of today, could be the breakthrough of tomorrow

Be patient, when you're ready, you're ready and not before

Be patient, when you are ready it will flow

Be patient, the flesh that needs to be added to the bones needs time to develop

Be patient, let your mind expel your words and thoughts with no expectation

Be patient, expectation builds frustration when the words don't come out right

Be patient, feed in positivity, belief and hope and the output will arrive

Be patient, the most beautiful of blooms need time to reach their full potential, also

Be patient, the most beautiful of blooms sometimes has to have had a lot of manure!

Be patient, record it, note it down, save it for later

Be patient, random parts and scraps of notes will fit together when the time is right

Be patient, when the time is right, the time is right and not before

Be patient, you were born to be courageously original

Be patient, capturing magic and inspiration takes skill and time

Be patient, tomorrow will arrive when the time is right

Be patient, inspiration has a habit of hiding if you chase it too hard

Be patient, back away, relax, depressurize

Be patient, relax, refuel, return

Be patient, when the time is right, the answers you need will be revealed

Be patient, if the answer you were expecting doesn't come, perhaps it wasn't your question

Be patient, if the answer you received wasn't right, perhaps it wasn't the right question

Be patient, rejection may not be a 'never', it may be just a 'not now'

Be patient, if it matters to you, you will find the time and effort to do it

Be patient, change takes time and planning

Be patient, rushing, achieves nothing, fast

Be patient, understanding takes time and experience

Be patient, 'Life' is not a destination

Be patient, if you have to have a 'checklist' of what you need to achieve

Be patient, sometimes the things on your checklist may take longer than you think, and

Be patient, if it takes longer, it takes longer and that is fine

Be patient, disappointments will fade

Be patient, failures are merely the stepping-stones to future success

Be patient, the bad times will pass, like storms clouds, they too will fade

Be patient, happiness will return, give it time, sunshine will arrive

Be patient, change is uncertainty and uncertainty will change

Be patient, the questions of today are the knowledge of tomorrow

Be patient, the knowledge of tomorrow can only be reached by passing through today

Be patient, you owe it to yourself, you can only be who you can be

Be patient, the person you are today is unique and beautiful

Be patient, the person you will be tomorrow will be even more informed than today

Be patient, improvement is continual, from day to day to day to day……..

Be patient, if it wasn't your turn today, it might be tomorrow

Be patient, yesterday was a teacher

Be patient, today is a gift

Be patient, tomorrow is only a promise

Be patient, some promises get broken no matter what you do

Be patient, when it's done, it's done and not before

Be patient, patience takes time and practice to learn

Be patient, sometimes patience isn't enough and that can be painful

Be patient, pain subsides and resilience will take its place

Be patient, resilience can grow to protect you from pain

Be patient, knowing *when* to change takes time

Be patient, change takes bravery

Be patient, bravery needs to be constructed, step by step

Be patient, when you're brave enough, you will change what you need to

Be patient, when you need to change, you *will know* when that time is

Be patient, you're doing so much better than you give yourself credit for

Be patient, you're so much stronger than you realise

Be patient, above everything else, always remember, be patient with yourself…..

Reap and Sow

We all want to be respected
We all want to be admired
We all want to be liked
Even if we don't admit it

We all need to respect others
Even if we don't like or admire them

We all need to respect others
Until we're given good reason not to

We need to give out what we want to receive
You reap what you sow, that's what you need to know

To give out to others, what you want to receive yourself
Is the best way you can show respect every single day

You reap what you sow, that's what you need to know

Comparisons

It's not that I am better, it's not that I am worse
In fact I'd have to say, that comparing is a curse

Compare yourself to others, there's one thing you'll discover
You may create divisions, from which you won't recover

Do it if you want, it won't do you any good
They'll only do it differently and that will boil your blood

It's better that they're them and it's better that you're you
If you just work together there's more that you can do

The comparing of some products that you may wish to buy
Yes that's perfect sense, that is something you should try

But us as human beings, to be different is quite key
It's important that you're you and I really must be me

Happiness and peace is all we want to find
It's easier to do if to others we are kind

So I wish you all the best, as you progress through your day
And others will be different and trust me, that's OK

Well that's my thoughts upon it, by all means don't agree
It's best that you are you and it's best that I am me

Journey Subject To Change

Finding Peace In Uncertainty

Finding peace there in uncertainty, is the only way to live
Sometimes we must receive and sometimes we need to give
We never know from day to day which way the pendulum ticks
But let me tell you now the best of all the tricks

Finding peace in the uncertainty will always see you through
Consider where you started from and all that you've been through
You never really knew what would greet you on your way
But all that you have been through has brought you to today

Finding peace in the uncertainty may not always be that easy
And whilst some of this sounds corny, and probably quite cheesy
The reason why these sayings stay, is because they tell the truth
You can never see the stars if you hide beneath the roof

Finding peace in the uncertainty will be a challenge that's for sure
But you'll never reach the future, if you won't open up the door
Take a moment of your time to review things of your past
By being brave before, it has brought you here at last

Finding peace in the uncertainty has worked for you before
You swam out in the sea when you couldn't see the shore
So at this very moment celebrate how far you've come
And stride on up the road to the sound of your own drum

Finding peace in the uncertainty is truly quite your thing
You didn't know the notes, but 'Oh wow!' how you did sing
Then slowly as you realise, that yes you can do this
You might just see that 'Lady Luck' she's giving you a kiss

Finding peace in the uncertainty, Oh yeah you've got this nailed
No-ones ever got success if at first they haven't failed
Crack on my friend, just stride out, you know you've got today
Put a smile upon your face and just be on your way

178

Journey Subject To Change

Finding peace in the uncertainty will never hold you back
You know that with your skills, the cards for you are stacked
And there you see, you know it, uncertainty's OK
I'm here and I'm alive, I'm gonna smash it all today…!

Everyone Deserves a Second Chance – That Includes You..!

Everyone deserves a second chance they say
But think for just a moment, have you had yours today?
Sometimes it's very easy, to give this thing to others
To give out all this kindness to friends, colleagues and brothers

Mistakes are only natural, and to others we give slack
But sometimes to ourselves, we constantly attack
So please just take a moment, give yourself a thought
Are you in unkind thinking of yourself constantly caught?

Perhaps if this is so, you might find that you are feeling
That from this constant battering, you're continually reeling
Yes I understand that you want to be your best
You try so very hard to make everyone impressed

But everyone needs time to recoup and to recover
By taking just a moment, you may well just discover
That you can go again, renewed and quite refreshed
And that you can do more than even you had guessed

So second chances, yes I'm in, dish them off the shelf
But first look in the mirror and give one to yourself..!

Ebb and Flow

Your peace is not my peace
Your balance and calm, is not mine
Where you feel happy and satisfied
Is different to where I feel happy and satisfied

This is the way of life
This is how it is supposed to be
This is how the world should work
This is right

Everyone needs what works for them
Everyone needs to feel safe
Everyone needs to feel happy
Everyone needs to be contented

But

For every single person these feelings come from a different set of circumstances
It isn't about all finding happiness in the exact same things, that is unrealistic

We each need to find our 'own' happy

And

Then we need to learn how to balance that, in conjunction with and in connection with, everyone else's happy

Our happy, whilst of the utmost importance to us, should not be sacrificed for, nor, be found at, the expense of others, but by working in harmony with others

As they give, we receive
As we give, they receive

Journey Subject To Change

Like breathing
In and out
In Balance
Each taking their turn
This is life

Kindness and balance
Give and take
Ebb and flow

Thankfulness

Today I'm being different in the things I choose to view

Here's a list of 'Thankfulness' could you produce one too…..?

Today I am thankful for……Back surgery
Yeah, that's a little different I will grant you that
But the trouble I experienced it really lay me flat
If it wasn't for the surgeon, God knows where I'd be
How's that for a start?…………That'll do for me.

Today I am thankful for……Tough times
Come on, be surprised, that wasn't as expected
I've had some really tough times, yeah my life has been infected
By going through the rubbish times, I can see when life is good
Sometimes with engine trouble you look beneath the hood.

Today I am thankful for…… Loss and what it teaches you
This one's really deep, but please let me explain
Losing someone special, is a truly agonising pain
There is a love you share, which at times is hard to see
But the one thing I can tell you, is they'll always be with me

Today I am thankful for…… Not being perfect
I know, who'd be so arrogant, to even think they were?
I never have……honestly! I'm sure that you'll concur
The joy in this is simple and this I can discern
Throughout this life of trials, there's always something you can learn

Today I am thankful for…… Family and Friends
Yes I know this one's a given, but it still has to be said
And families sometimes, they can get right in your head
They can push all the right buttons to really get to you
But family and friends, they really see you through

Journey Subject To Change

Today I am thankful for…… Work and earning a salary
Now this one's controversial, or it could be, let's just see
Work can be a challenge, or is that only me?
Work it changes day to day, back and forth from good to bad
And whilst not paid enough, of some money I am glad

Today I am thankful for…… The ability to reason things through
It sounds a little convoluted, but again let me expand
Life and trials and tribulations, they just go hand in hand
And if you're very lucky, like today I think I am….
You can see both good and bad and hope that there's a plan

Today I am thankful for……The ability to be thankful at all
There are many things within this world that can test the best of us
War and hate, injustice……….the crashing of a bus
Many more that could be listed but we all know what I mean
And that is why to celebrate, 'Thankfulness', I'm keen

Music, words, sunshine, rain, snow and all the flowers
If I try and think of it, I could go on for hours

Love, compassion, kindness, the skill of other people
Children, joy, laughter, a church with its fine steeple

Little things and big things, they all count to the score
All you have to do sometimes, is just look out for more

Diversity and difference and also sport as well
When looking at my 'Thankfulness' it makes my heart to swell

Well, only metaphorically, it just helps me feel quite glad
I use it here and there to disappear the sad

As I said right at the start, 'Thankfulness' is in my view
If you really need it, it will be there for you

Journey Subject To Change

Please don't get me wrong, sometimes it isn't easy
There are days that for no reason they aren't that bright and breezy

Start a simple list, just a word or two will do
Save it down and then return it's always there for you

As you build upon it, the list will grow and grow
And when you really need it, it might just help you so

Cats, kittens, birdsong, a dog, a stream, some woods
Ice cream, chocolate, cheese, a tray of some baked goods

It's your list now, it isn't mine, so do just as you please
I'll leave you with the final lines and pass to you the keys....

As I leave, if you're still here, at the end of this long rhyme
Then that is yet another thing, I'm 'Thankful' for your time.......

Tears Are Not Weakness

Tears are not weakness
Muscles are not strength
I know in life sometimes
It just doesn't make much sense

But tears are not weakness
They're a message from your soul
It's good to show your feelings
As it helps to keep you whole

Tears are essential
You have to let them flow
It helps your inner being
To let the feelings go

If something really matters
And tears have to fall
Then deep inside it's like
Your spirit's made a call

It's called upon your heart
To say 'this' really matters
If we cannot let it out
Then inside we'll be in tatters

Please don't be embarrassed
These feelings you must process
Do not keep them deep inside
And feed them like a hostess

To keep them deep inside
Helps them fester and grow bad
And this I guarantee you
Will only make you sad

Journey Subject To Change

So tears are not weakness
They're a system of filtration
Like water's really good for you
It's sort of like hydration

It flushes out the things
That have to be let go
If the tears start to fall
Then please just let them flow....

What Price Wisdom?

I had reason to consider
Today for quite some time
If my days had been spent wisely
Or did I commit a crime?

I looked around my history
To try and calculate a score
To see how I was doing
Could I have done some more?

Were the days I spent in anguish
Really worth the price?
Had the worry I had wasted
Made me live the bad times twice?

First of all you worry
About the thing to come
And then when it arrives
You'll add a second to the sum

I considered for a moment
The sum of the equation
I decided that indeed
This thing was worth a-raisin'

So yes, there will be times
When things be on your mind
But this here is your wisdom
To yourself you must be kind……

Days of Daze

If it wasn't for tomorrow
Today would not exist
If it wasn't for your yesterday
You'd know not what you'd missed

Tomorrow is a promise
That today cannot fulfill
And yesterday it was
A long forgotten thrill

Tomorrow never comes
Today that's what they say
Yesterday was fun
But that has gone away

Tomorrow is a goal
That today we must strive for
Yesterday our view
Was of a different door

Tomorrow we'll look back
On today, a day we feared
Then yesterday will be
A day that should be cheered

Tomorrow is a word
And today is just a phase
The yesterday's we lived
Are now our daze of days

Phases, Crazes and Mazes

Life is never ever one thing
It's a mish-mash mixed up plot
One day you've got it all together
And there's others when you've not

So let's establish one thing
Change will happen anyway
Accept that this is so
And you're truly on your way

There was this funky pop-star
I thought he was the biz
So 'hot', yet cool and trendy
I wished my life was his

My hair was done all punk
I wore make-up on my face
I think I looked just like a fool
But I thought that I was ace

Now that there was a 'phase'
I soon grew out of that
And when I see the pictures
I look just like a prat

Then there was this cube-thing
Different colours on all sides
I heard that if you did it quick
Then you might just win a prize

Most of us we had one
When I was just a kid
Mine I think was second-hand
I bought it for a quid

Journey Subject To Change

Now this thing, it was a 'craze'
It swept through everywhere
I always had it in my hand
For other things I didn't care

You go through different things
Different 'phases' in your life
And if you're truly lucky
You'll find a partner, husband, wife

You may eat certain foods
You might exercise a lot
You might like a certain artist
Because they're 'super-hot'

And then you may decide
That these things are not for you
You liked them at the time
But it's just a 'craze' you're through

Then you might discover
As through different things you pass
The things that really matter
They 'kind of' tend to last

You may also start to see
New things come into focus
And life is truly magic
When you get some 'hocus-pocus'

It's also at this time
As life drives you round the bend
You learn that life's a 'maze'
And you cannot see the end

Journey Subject To Change

You might set out on your journey
With a destination set
But there is no guarantee
That, that is where you'll get

So if you start to realise
That your life has been through 'phases'
Then you start to understand
The whole things 'crazy mazes'

Keep belief in what you're doing
If you think that, that is right
Never be afraid to shine
We all have our own light

If things don't seem straightforward
Just at this current time
It may well be as written
As you've read now in my rhyme

It could well be a 'craze'
And this thing is not for you
Or it might just be a 'phase'
That you have to pass on through

Don't lose your faith or focus
Keep believing please my friend
Just remember life's a 'maze'
And we just can't see the end

Work In Progress

Please excuse my appearance, I'm not my best today
Be careful where you tread as work is underway
I can't give any timescale for how long the work will last
But given my experience from the things within my past
I believe the work is scheduled to be lasting for a while
It could well be, still on-going, even when I smile

So I'm grateful for your patience and your understanding
Although I cannot guarantee, how rude comments will be landing
I'd appreciate your help and your consideration
By avoiding nasty words that could lead to confrontation
I hope you understand though, this applies to all of us
We're trying hard to be our best and not to cause a fuss

None of us gets all things right, every single day
If you believe you do, then you'd best be on your way
That isn't realistic, it just cannot be the truth
If you believe it is, then all I'll say is "Strewth!"
We're just trying very hard to be our very best
Some days we get it right, some days it is a test

This cuts both ways I know it's so, so I'll be gentle back
If we treat each other kindly, perhaps we'll stay on track
So as we pass each other by, or as we share a conversation
We're all just trains upon our way and visiting each station
I am a work in progress and I know that you are too
If we look out for each other, perhaps we'll make it through

Journey Subject To Change

Ticket Not Valid for Travel

I never really realised
I wonder if you do?
That when a seed is sown
A ticket's given too…..

You never even see it
You can't hold it in your hand
But everyone possesses one
And each journey has been planned

All journeys differ greatly
Some are long and some quite short
Some they are straightforward
And others twist as they contort

The strangest thing of all
Is they're all a mystery trip
No-one ever really knows
When off it they do skip

Some journeys last and last
For decades end on end
Some journeys hardly start
They come off at the first bend

No matter what their distance
The destination is the same
And getting there quite quickly
I guarantee is not your aim

The magic lies within the travel
Ease and comfort is the key
Take the time to stop a while
As there's many things to see

Journey Subject To Change

Take the route that's picturesque
I think would be my tip
Avoiding the conductor
So your ticket he can't clip

The validation of your ticket
That happens at the start
As the purchase confirmation
Is done straight from the heart

You don't take any luggage
You get baggage on the way
But try and travel light
Is the one thing I would say

You'll encounter other passengers
Some will join you on your trip
Others come and go
And there's some you'd rather skip

But the journey isn't like that
Things will happen as they will
The best that you can hope for
Is to navigate with skill

Some days will be good
And some they will unravel
You just don't want to hear
"This ticket's not for travel..!"

Check on your itinerary
Well, the one you try and plan
It starts out as a mystery
But sometimes it hits the fan

Journey Subject To Change

Diversions, missed connections
They're all part of the scheme
And don't pull funny faces
Or you'll end up as a 'meme'

The key thing to remember
And I can't stress this enough
Be kind, caring and helpful
But beneath that just stay tough

The final thing above all else
Is to do what *you* must do
Take advice and listen
But this journey's just for you

The End

That my friend is the end of this part of your journey, you've read it all (hopefully!).

However, who wants to end with something boring, I certainly don't and I'm hoping that neither do you.

There is *ONE* thing, just *ONE*, that has made all the difference in getting to this point of the book. Luckily I am able to provide the answer to what that thing is.

YOU

Never forget that it is *YOU* who makes anything and indeed, everything possible.

I can't guarantee you that whatever it is you want to achieve is easy, but, I can guarantee you that the only way you get there is if *YOU* decide you want to do it.

Always Remember.

YOU are the *most important factor* in achieving anything you want to achieve.

I hope that your journey may have been slightly altered for the better having read this book, and knowing that you are not alone and that you will get there.

Onwards and upwards brave traveller!!

Your next adventure awaits you.

Printed in Great Britain
by Amazon